WordTips

Word 2010 Indexes and Special Tables

Compiled from the pages of WordTips, *your free weekly productivity newsletter*

tips .NET

Word 2010 Indexes and Special Tables

Published by:

Sharon Parq Associates, Inc.
PO Box 794
Orem, UT 84059

For information on purchasing, distributing, or reselling books published by Sharon Parq Associates, Inc., please visit our website (www.SharonParq.com) or call 801-607-2035. Our books are also available through select online resellers such as Amazon.com.

ISBN: 978-1-61359-052-2 (e-book on CD-ROM)
ISBN: 978-1-61359-053-9 (e-book)
ISBN: 978-1-61359-054-6 (printed book)

Produced and published in the United States of America

Revision history:

6 July 2011: First published

Table of Contents

Introduction ix

A Word about Word Versions x

Need More Tips? x

A Special Note of Thanks xi

Sharing this Document xi

Working with Index Entries 1

Creating an Index Entry 1

Creating an Index Entry for a Range of Pages 3

Cross-Referencing Index Entries 4

Deleting Index Entries 6

Specifying Sub-entries in an AutoMark File 6

Adding Quoted Words to an Index 8

Creating Indexes 11

Creating a Normal Index 11

Indexing a Range of Pages 13

Indexing Based on a Range of Letters 13

Multiple Indexes in a Document 14

Putting Your Index after Your Endnotes 16

Improper Index References 19

Formatting an Index 21

Inconsistent Formatting in an Index 21

Putting Bold Words in an Index 22

Improper Index Page Numbers 27
Specifying Index Section Dividers 29
Specifying an Index Entry Separator 30
Specifying an Index Page-Range Separator 30
Including Section Numbers in an Index 31
Chapter Numbers in Indexes and TOAs 32

Tables of Contents from Headings 37
Creating a Table of Contents from Heading Levels 37
Controlling the Number of Heading Levels in a TOC 38
Creating a TOC that Includes Specific Styles 40
Problems with TOC Styles 43

Tables of Contents from Fields 45
Specifying a Table of Contents Entry 45
Creating a Table of Contents from TOC Fields 46
Two-Line Headings in a TOC 48
Using TC Fields for Notes 49

Table of Contents Gallery 51
Inserting a Preformatted Table of Contents 51
Adding a TOC to the Table of Contents Gallery 52

Formatting a Table of Contents 55
Creating a TOC without Hyperlinks 55
Adding Column Headings to a Table of Contents 56
Creating an Inline Heading 57
Customized Tables of Contents 58
TOC Heading Numbers Always Show in Bold 60

Table of Contents Tricks 63
Page Ranges in a TOC 63
Two Types of Page Numbers in a TOC 63
Using Multiple Tables of Contents 64
Insert a TOC without Upsetting Pagination 67
Generating a TOC that Includes Text Boxes 67
Locking Lines in a TOC 68

Deleting a Table of Contents 69
Updating an Entire TOC from a Macro 70

Creating a Table of Authorities 73
Creating a Table of Authorities 73
Generating a Table of Authorities 74
Creating Categories for Your Table of Authorities 76
Ensuring Proper Page Numbers for a Table of Authorities 77

Other Special Tables 79
Auto Creation of an Acronym List 79
Creating Usable Figure Captions 83
Turning Off Figure Caption Numbering 83
Overriding Automatic Numbering of Tables 84
Table Numbers are Skipped 85

Introduction

Use Word for just a short time, and you quickly discover that the program provides dozens of different tools you can use to create special elements for your documents. Some of these elements are designed to make your documents—particularly longer documents—easier for readers to use. Chief among these elements are indexes and special tables.

Word includes a complete indexing system that gives you a marvelous level of control over how your index is constructed. It also includes a variety of special tables that can provide a framework for different parts of your document. The most common of these is a table of contents, although other tables (such as a table of authorities) can be easily added.

Word 2010 Indexes and Special Tables can help you make sense of not only these document elements, but also the tools that Word puts at your disposal to create the elements. This e-book is what you need to master these tools and create the index or special table that you need. Information is presented in bite-sized tips gathered from the pages of the ***WordTips*** newsletters over the years. Taken as a whole, these tips can help you make indexes and special tables a regular part of your document creation process.

There are dozens of tips in this book, each explaining a different facet of working with indexes, tables of contents, or other types of special tables. The tips are organized into chapters, as noted in the Table of Contents. You can either read through an entire chapter of your choosing, or you can simply reference the exact tip that will address what you are trying to do.

A Word about Word Versions

As the title of this e-book implies, ***Word 2010 Indexes and Special Tables*** is designed to work with Word 2010. The reason is simple: The latest release of Microsoft's word processing program has operational differences—some subtle and some major—from earlier versions of Word. These differences can affect the way that you create and work with indexes and special tables in the program.

The instructions and screen shots used in this e-book were all created using a Windows 7 system with Word 2010 installed. As you compare what is on your screen with what you see in this e-book, don't be surprised if there are small, cosmetic differences. If you run across discrepancies of a more serious nature (I don't think you will), I'd love you to e-mail me with the details. Send your message to allen@sharonparq.com.

Word has long included the tools discussed in this e-book; they are not new with Word 2010. If you are using an earlier version of Word and you want to discover how to work efficiently and effectively with indexes and special tables in your version of the program, check the Tips.Net store and you can find a version of this e-book designed specifically for you.

Need More Tips?

Remember that this document contains many tips presented in ***past*** issues of ***WordTips***. If you want to stay at the top of your Word form, you should consider subscribing to ***WordTips***. All you need is an e-mail account, and you can receive a weekly dose of tips related to Word. To subscribe to the version of ***WordTips*** that is right for you, visit this Web site:

`http://wordribbon.tips.net`

Don't forget that ***WordTips*** is part of the Tips.Net network, where you can find thousands of tips on a wide variety of topics.

`http://www.tips.net`

A Special Note of Thanks

I would like to thank the many thousands of past and current ***WordTips*** subscribers. Without their assistance, many of these tips would not have been possible. Week in and week out I receive e-mail from people needing help, as well as from people willing to offer help. These people selflessly provide assistance to others, submitting solutions to problems that others face.

Sharing this Document

A lot of work went into putting this e-book together. I can't tell you how many countless hours are spent putting together the weekly ***WordTips*** newsletter from which this information was compiled. That means that this information has value, and your friends, neighbors, and co-workers may want to share it.

The information in this e-book is copyrighted. Please do not share this information with others—you purchased ***Word 2010 Indexes and Special Tables,*** and you have a right to use it on your system. Another person who has not purchased this e-book does not have that right. It is the sales of this valuable information that makes the continued publishing of ***WordTips*** possible. If enough people disregard that simple economic fact, the newsletter will no longer be viable or available.

If your friends think this information is valuable enough to ask you for it, they should think it is valuable enough to purchase on their own. After all, the price is low enough that just about anyone should be able to afford it.

It should go without saying that you cannot post this document or the information it contains on any electronic bulletin board, Web site, FTP site, newsgroup, or … well, you get the idea. The only place from which this document should be available is the ***WordTips*** Web site. If you want an original copy, visit the Tips. Net Store at the following address:

```
http://store.tips.net
```

1

Working with Index Entries

Creating an Index Entry

Word includes a feature that allows you to automatically create an index for your document. How you create the actual index is explained in a different tip, but first you must insert index entries throughout your document. These entries are used by Word to pull together the information that is placed in the index. To create an index entry, follow these steps:

1. Select the text you wish to appear as the index entry.
2. Press **ALT+SHIFT+X**. Word displays the Mark Index Entry dialog box.

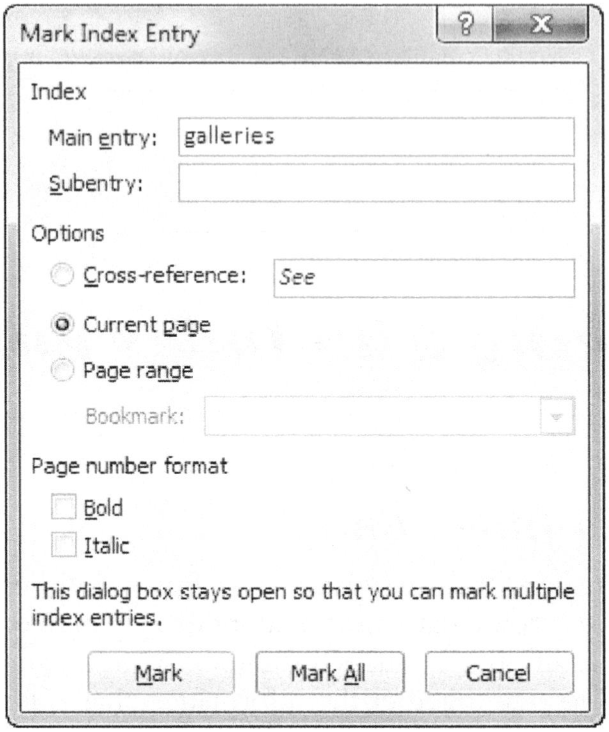

The Mark Index Entry dialog box.

3. Click on Mark.
4. If you want to mark additional index entries, select them in your document, and then click on Mark.
5. Click on Close to dismiss the Mark Index Entry dialog box.

Word also allows you to create index subentries. These are index entries that are subordinate to other index entries, and generally appear indented under the main index entry. To insert an index subentry, follow these steps:

1. Select the text you wish to appear as the subentry.
2. Press **Alt+Shift+X**. Word displays the Mark Index Entry dialog box. Notice that the text you selected is shown in the Main Entry text box.
3. Press **Ctrl+C** to copy the selected Main Entry text to the Clipboard.

4. Position the insertion point in the Subentry text box.
5. Press **Ctrl+V** to paste the text into the Subentry text box.
6. Change the information in the Main Entry text box to indicate the main index entry to which this subentry should be subordinate.
7. Click on Mark.
8. Click on Close to dismiss the Mark Index Entry dialog box.

Creating an Index Entry for a Range of Pages

If you have ever created an index before, you know that it is possible for an index reference to refer to a range of pages. Word makes this type of index entry easy through the use of bookmarks. To do this, follow these steps:

1. Select the text you want to use as the range of pages in the index. This text may span several pages.
2. Assign a bookmark to this text selection.
3. Press **Alt+Shift+X** to display the Mark Index Entry dialog box.

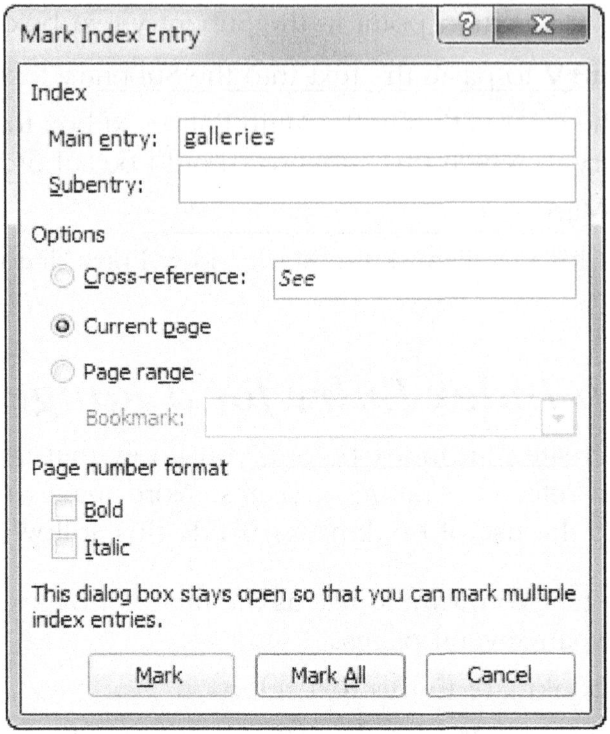

The Mark Index Entry dialog box.

4. In the Main Entry text box, enter the index entry as you want it to appear in the index.
5. Select the Page Range radio button.
6. Use the drop-down Bookmark list to select the name of the bookmark you defined in step 2.
7. Click on Mark.
8. Repeat steps 4 through 7, as desired.
9. Click on Close to dismiss the Mark Index Entry dialog box.

Cross-Referencing Index Entries

Creating index entries in a Word document is easy, as you learn in other ***WordTips.*** It is not uncommon to cross-reference items in an index, and such cross-references require a change in how you create the index entries. For instance, instead of page numbers after an entry, you might have the text ***See Johnson, Abigail.*** To insert a cross-reference in an index entry, follow these steps:

1. Select the text you wish to appear as the main index entry. This is the text under which the cross reference will appear.
2. Press **ALT+SHIFT+X**. Word displays the Mark Index Entry dialog box. Notice that the Main Entry text box is already filled in with the text you specified in step 1.

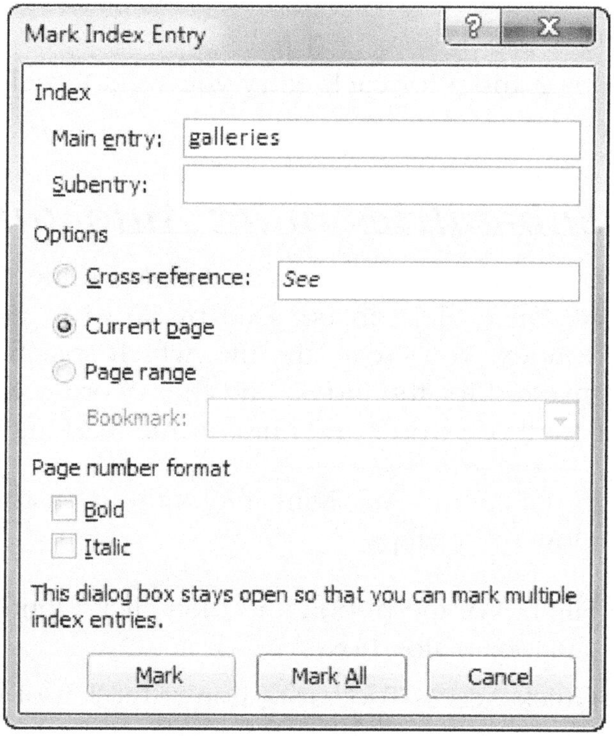

The Mark Index Entry dialog box.

3. Select the Cross-reference radio button.
4. In the text box to the right of the Cross-reference radio button, enter the cross reference, as you want it to appear.
5. Click on Mark.
6. Click on Close to dismiss the Mark Index Entry dialog box.

Deleting Index Entries

Word provides the tools for you to create complete indexes for your documents. After creating all the index entries, as described in other ***WordTips,*** you might decide later to remove an index entry. To do this, follow these general steps:

1. Make sure you have Word set to display text that is formatted as hidden.
2. Use Find and Replace (**Ctrl+F**) to locate the index entry you want to delete.
3. Select the entire field, including the field braces, and press **Del**. The index entry is deleted.
4. Repeat steps 2 and 3 for each entry you want to delete.

Specifying Sub-entries in an AutoMark File

John asked how to specify sub-entries in an AutoMark file. An AutoMark file, also called a concordance file, can be used by Word to automatically mark a document for an index. You create the file, which specifies what words or phrases you want marked for the index, and then Word searches through the document, looking for those words and phrases and marking them accordingly.

There is no way to utilize and AutoMark file without customizing the Quick Access Toolbar. Follow these steps:

1. Click the File tab of the ribbon and then click Options. Word displays the Word Options dialog box.
2. Click the Quick Access Toolbar option at the left of the dialog box.

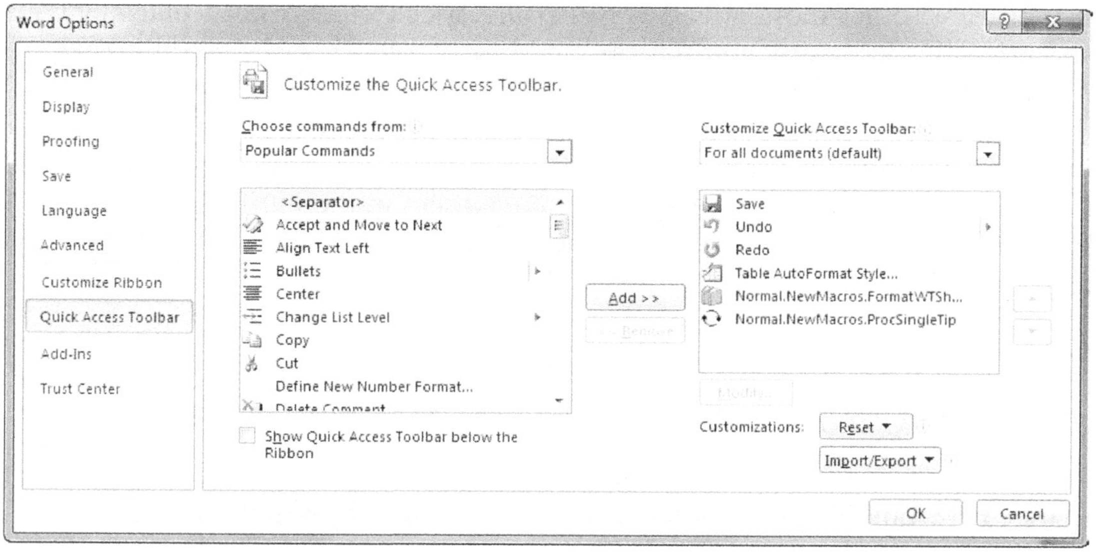

The Quick Access Toolbar options of the Word Options dialog box.

3. Using the Choose Commands From drop-down list, choose Commands Not In the Ribbon. Word adjusts the commands available at the left side of the dialog box.
4. Scroll through the list of commands and click once on the Index and Tables command.
5. Click the Add button. The Index and Tables command moves to the right side of the dialog box.
6. Click OK. The dialog box disappears, and a green dot (the Index and Tables command) appears on the Quick Access Toolbar.

Now, if you click on the Index and Options dot, you will see the Index and Options dialog box and you can click the AutoMark button within that dialog box.

Basically, an AutoMark file consists of a two-column table. In the left-hand column you specify the word or phrase that you want to trigger an index entry. In the right-hand column you specify the actual index entry itself. For instance, in the left-hand column you might enter Menkaure, and in the right column you might enter Pyramids. In this way, every occurrence of the word Menkaure in your document would result in an index entry under the word Pyramids.

If you want to get more specific, you could specify that a particular keyword should go under a subentry. For instance, you could put the word Menkaure in the left-hand column, and in the right you could put Pyramids:Egypt. In this way, every instance of the word Menkaure in your document would result in an index entry under the word Egypt, which is a sub-entry to the word Pyramids. Likewise, you could put Teotihuachuan in the left-hand column and Pyramids:Mexico in the right, and every instance of Teotihuachuan is marked as n index entry under Mexico, which is under Pyramids.

Adding Quoted Words to an Index

Mike has a document that contains quite a few words surrounded by quote marks. He would like the quoted words to be marked for inclusion in an index and for the quote marks to be removed.

The best way to make such a change in your document is through the use of a macro. The macro needs to search for the quoted text, figure out where it starts and stops, delete the quote marks, and then add the index mark. (The mark is added through the use of an XE field.)

There are probably many ways that such a macro could be constructed. The following is one that could be used:

```
Sub QuotesToIndexEntries()
    Dim iOpenQuote As Integer
    Dim iCloseQuote As Integer
    Dim sP As String
    Dim sPhrase As String
    Dim iParas As Integer

    If Selection.ExtendMode Then Exit Sub

    iParas = Selection.Paragraphs.Count
    Selection.StartOf unit:=wdParagraph, Extend:=wdMove
    For J = 1 To iParas
        Selection.MoveEnd unit:=wdParagraph
        sP = Selection.Text
        iOpenQuote = InStr(sP, Chr(34))
        If iOpenQuote = 0 Then iOpenQuote = InStr(sP, Chr(147))
```

```
        While iOpenQuote > 0
            iCloseQuote = InStr(iOpenQuote + 1, sP, Chr(34))
            If iCloseQuote = 0 Then
                iCloseQuote = InStr(iOpenQuote + 1, sP, Chr(148))
            End If
            If iCloseQuote > 0 Then
                sPhrase = Mid(sP, iOpenQuote + 1, _
                  iCloseQuote - iOpenQuote - 1)
                Selection.Collapse Direction:=wdCollapseStart
                Selection.MoveRight unit:=wdCharacter, _
                  Count:=iOpenQuote - 1, Extend:=wdMove
                Selection.Delete unit:=wdCharacter, Count:=1
                Selection.MoveRight unit:=wdCharacter, _
                  Count:=Len(sPhrase), Extend:=wdMove
                Selection.Delete unit:=wdCharacter, Count:=1

                Selection.Fields.Add Range:=Selection.Range, _
                  Type:=wdFieldEmpty, _
                  PreserveFormatting:=False
                Selection.MoveLeft unit:=wdCharacter, Count:=1
                Selection.Delete unit:=wdCharacter, Count:=2
                Selection.TypeText Text:="XE " + Chr(34) + _
                  sPhrase + Chr(34)
                Selection.MoveRight unit:=wdCharacter, _
                  Count:=1, Extend:=wdMove
            End If
            Selection.MoveEnd unit:=wdParagraph
            sP = Selection.Text
            iOpenQuote = InStr(sP, Chr(34))
            If iOpenQuote = 0 Then iOpenQuote = InStr(sP, Chr(147))
        Wend

        Selection.MoveStart unit:=wdParagraph, Count:=1
    Next J
End Sub
```

In order to use the macro, just select the text you want to affect prior to running it. (If you want to affect the entire document, press **Ctrl+A** before running the macro.)

2

Creating Indexes

Creating a Normal Index

Once you have inserted all your index entries and subentries, Word allows you to create a complete index by following these steps:

1. Position the insertion point where you want the index inserted.
2. Display the References tab of the ribbon.
3. In the Index group click the Insert Index tool. Word displays the Index dialog box.

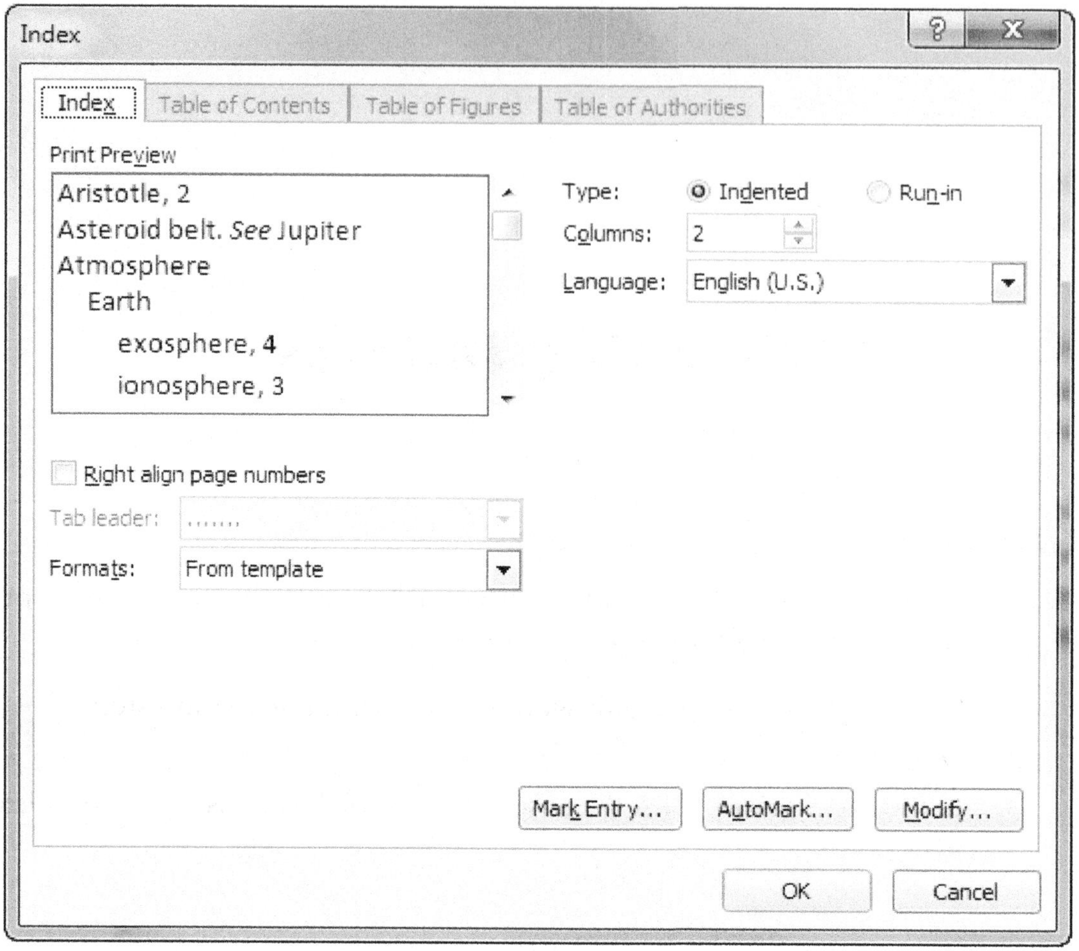

The Index tab of the Index dialog box.

4. Use the controls in the dialog box to indicate how you want the index to appear.
5. Click on OK.

Alternatively, you can follow these steps to create a normal index:

1. Position the insertion point where you want the index inserted.
2. Press **Ctrl+F9** to insert field brackets. Make sure the insertion point stays between the brackets.
3. Type **index**.

4. Press **F9** to update the field information. Word replaces the field with the index when the document is printed.

If you decide to use the index field to create your index, there are quite a few field switches you can use to control how Word creates the index. The most useful of these switches are discussed elsewhere in this e-book.

Indexing a Range of Pages

Word allows you to create indexes for your documents easily and quickly. Once you create your index entries and subentries (using fields), you can create an index for a range of pages by following these steps:

1. Select (highlight) the pages you want to include in the index.
2. Assign a bookmark to this text.
3. Place the insertion point at the location where you want the partial index created.
4. Press **Ctrl+F9** to insert field brackets. Make sure the insertion point stays between the brackets.
5. Type **index \b** followed by the name of the bookmark used in step 2.
6. Press **F9** to update the field information. Word replaces the field with the partial index.

Indexing Based on a Range of Letters

Word allows you to create indexes for your documents easily and quickly. Once you've created the index entries and subentries in the document, you can create an index for a range of letters by following these steps:

1. Place the insertion point at the location in your document where you want the partial index created.
2. Press **Ctrl+F9** to insert field brackets. Make sure the insertion point stays between the brackets.

3. Type **index \p** followed by the range of letters for which you want an index. For instance, you could type **index \p D-R** to specify you only wanted an index created for index entries beginning with the letters *D–R*, inclusive.
4. Press **F9** to update the field information. Word replaces the field with the partial index.

Multiple Indexes in a Document

Marc has a multi-sectioned document. He wants to create an index on one section and a second index for the entire document. Marc wonders if there is a way to have two indexes in a document where one of them covers only a single section.

The short answer is yes, there is a way. When you insert an index into a document, what you are actually doing is inserting the INDEX field. With no switches used in the field, Word creates an index based on the entire document. To create an index based on only a portion of the document (such as on a single section), follow these general steps:

1. Select the document section that you want to have indexed in its own special index.
2. Create a bookmark that applies to the selected text. (Click the Bookmark tool on the Insert tab of the ribbon.) Remember the name you used for the bookmark.
3. Create the basic INDEX field. (Press **Ctrl+F9** to insert field braces and type the word INDEX.)
4. After the word INDEX, type a space, **\b** (to indicate that this index will apply to only a bookmarked area of the text), another space, and the name of the bookmark you created in step 2. Your entire field should look something like this:

```
{ INDEX \b MySection }
```

5. Press **F9** to collapse the field and create your index.

There is another way to approach the problem, as well: You could add a switch to the XE field that is used to create an index entry. For instance, let's say you are indexing the term "polar bear" for the index. Make sure you have a field near the term like this one:

```
{ XE "polar bear" \f "a" }
```

The \f switch should appear only for index entries in the section that you want to have its own index. Later, when you insert the INDEX field to create the index for that section, you should make sure it looks like this:

```
{ INDEX \f "a" }
```

The index created by this field will only included those index entries that use the \f switch followed by the number 1.

Adding the switch to the XE fields is handy, but suppose that you've already created your index entries without using the \f switch. If you want to later add the \f switch to the XE fields in the section, you can do it by following these steps:

1. Type **\f "a"** (note the space in there) in a blank spot of your document and then cut it to the Clipboard.
2. Make sure that field codes are displayed in your document. (Press **Alt+F9** to either show or hide the field codes.)
3. Select all the text in the section that will have its own index.
4. Press **Ctrl+H** to display the Replace tab of the Find and Replace dialog box.
5. In the Find box, type **XE "*"**
6. In the Replace box, type **^&**, a space, and then **^c**. The **^&** will replace what is found with itself, then there's a space, and the **^c** adds what is on the Clipboard (from Step 1).
7. Click More and make sure the Use Wildcards checkbox is selected.
8. Click Replace All. When you're asked if you want to search the rest of the document, answer negatively. (You don't want to search the entire document; you only want to affect the portion you selected in step 3.)

You can find additional information about these steps in the Microsoft Knowledge Base:

```
http://support.microsoft.com/?kbid=154025
```

Putting Your Index after Your Endnotes

When you start adding different elements to your documents, you may wonder how to order those elements. For instance, Word allows you to easily add elements such as tables of contents, other special tables, footnotes, endnotes, and indexes. If your document contains both endnotes and an index, you may wonder how you can place your index after your endnotes.

The reason for this confusion typically crops up because Word allows you to specify where your endnotes are placed—at the end of a section or the end of the document. You obviously don't want the endnotes at the end of your document if you want your index to appear after the endnotes. So, the solution is to add a "next page" section break after the end of your document's body and just before the index. Your document should now contain two sections—one for the body of the document and one for the index. So, in the main body of the document format your endnotes so that they appear at the end of the section. You can do that by following these steps:

1. Position the insertion point within the section that contains your endnotes (the main body of your document).
2. Make sure the References tab of the ribbon is displayed.
3. Click the small icon at the bottom-right of the Footnotes group. Word displays the Footnote and Endnote dialog box.
4. Click the Endnotes radio button.

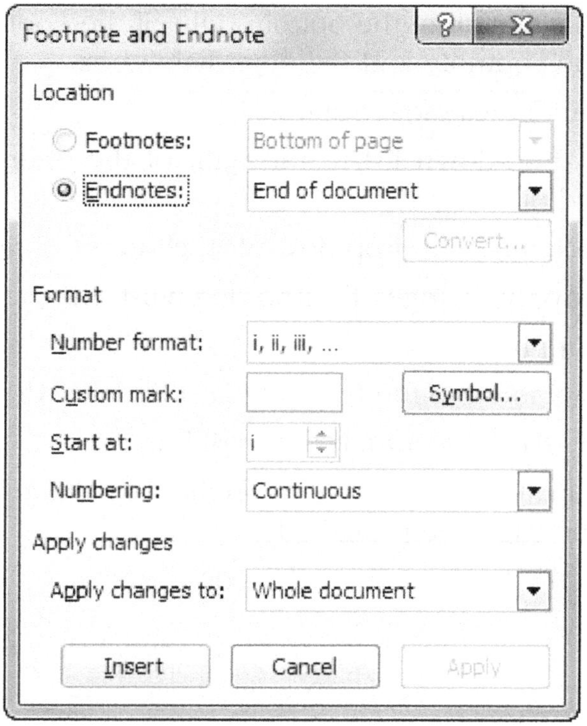

The Footnote and Endnote dialog box.

5. Using the drop-down list to the right of the Endnotes radio button, choose End of Section.
6. Click the Apply button.
7. Click Cancel to close the Footnote and Endnote dialog box.

Word then automatically places the endnotes before your index, just as you want.

Of course, if you are already using multiple sections in your document, then this simple approach won't work as you expect. You can still place your endnotes where you want, however:

1. Place the "next page" section break just before your index, as described earlier in this tip.
2. Make sure the References tab of the ribbon is displayed.

3. Click the small icon at the bottom-right of the Footnotes group. Word displays the Footnote and Endnote dialog box.
4. Click the Endnotes radio button.
5. Using the drop-down list to the right of the Endnotes radio button, choose End of Section.
6. Using the Numbering drop down list, choose Continuous.
7. Using the Apply Changes To drop-down list, choose Whole Document.
8. Click the Apply button.
9. Click Cancel to close the Footnote and Endnote dialog box.
10. Display the Page Layout tab of the ribbon.
11. Click the small icon at the bottom-right of the Page Setup group. Word displays the Page Setup dialog box.
12. Make sure the Layout tab is selected.

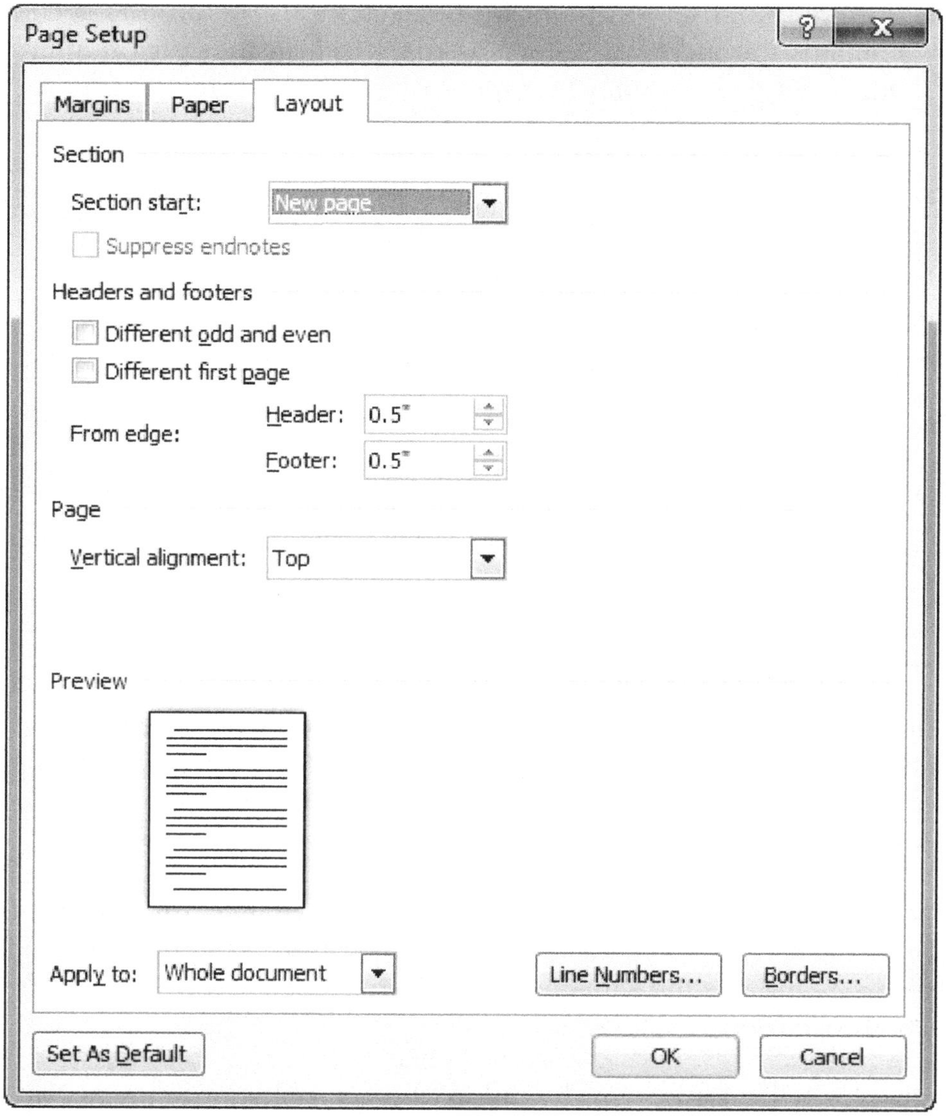

The Layout tab of the Page Setup dialog box.

13. Choose the Suppress Endnotes check box. (The check box is only accessible if two conditions are met: There are actually endnotes in your document and you've set the endnotes to appear at the end of the section instead of the end of the document.)
14. Using the Apply To drop-down list, choose Whole Document.
15. Click on OK.

16. Position the insertion point in the section just before the section that contains the index. (In other words, put it in the section after which you want the endnotes to appear.)
17. Display the Page Layout tab of the ribbon.
18. Click the small icon at the bottom-right of the Page Setup group. Word displays the Page Setup dialog box.
19. Make sure the Layout tab is selected.
20. Clear the Suppress Endnotes checkbox.
21. Using the Apply To drop-down list, choose This Section.
22. Click on OK.

Word suppresses the endnotes for all the sections except the one you specified (in step 16), so all your endnotes appear there—just before your index.

Improper Index References

Katherine wrote to indicate that she has some problems creating an index where the same term is indexed on page i and page 1 or on page ii and page 2. If the indexed term is on page i and page 2, there is no problem; the problem only exists when the page numbers are counterparts of each other.

From what I can tell, Word is designed to behave like this. As far as the program is concerned, there are duplicate page numbers in the document (i is the same as 1, and ii is the same as 2), so Word thinks that one page reference covers both occurrences.

Normally, this behavior by Word wouldn't be a problem. Commonly accepted page numbering practices use lowercase Roman numerals to paginate front matter or introductory matter. In the publishing world, front matter is seldom—if ever—indexed. Instead, the main body of the manuscript is indexed, and sometimes the appendices.

The only way around this behavior by Word is to take a look at the structure of your document, and consider moving any indexable content to the main body of the document—to page numbers where you use Arabic numerals.

3

Formatting an Index

Inconsistent Formatting in an Index

Don wrote a book using Word. Following the text is the index. The index is about 20 pages long and looks fine, except that Don is getting a few index entries appearing as bold text, perhaps 10 entries in total throughout the 20 index pages. He doesn't want them bold and has no idea why they are. If Don right-clicks on the entry and removes the bold it looks fine, but after he rebuilds the index by updating the field the bold reappears—always on the same 10 or so items. The related text in the body of the document is not bold. Don has deleted the words in the text, then rebuilt the index to eliminate that entry, then carefully re-typed the text in the manuscript making sure it is not bold. Sure enough, it becomes bold again in the index.

The give-away in this description is that the bold appears when the index is rebuilt. This means that there is a problem with the field codes used to mark index entries in the document. Here's what you should do, in general terms:

1. Locate the XE field code for the index entry. (You may need to enable the display of hidden text in order to see the location of the XE fields.)
2. Expand the entry so that you can see the underlying code.
3. Select the entire field code (including the braces) and press **Ctrl+Spacebar**. This sets the code back to normal, default font characteristics.

4. Make sure the XE field does not contain the \b switch. If it does, delete it.
5. Collapse the XE field again.

It is also possible that one of the styles used for indexing (Index 1, Index 2, etc.) are set to bold and not regular text. To determine if that is the case, examine what styles are used in the offending index entries and then modify those styles to reflect how you want the text to appear.

Putting Bold Words in an Index

Mori has a document that has "keywords" listed in boldface. He would like to create an index that includes these keywords. Mori wonders if there is a way to automatically mark all the bold phrases so they will appear in an index.

There are a couple of ways you can approach this task. Perhaps the easiest way is to take advantage of Word's AutoMark capability to create your index entries. The trick is to get your words—the ones you want into an index—into their own file. Here's an easy way to do that:

1. Open the document for which you want the index.
2. Create a new, blank document.
3. Switch back to your source document (the one for which you want the index).
4. Display the Home tab of the ribbon.
5. Click the Find tool, in the Editing group, and then choose Advanced Find. Word displays the Find tab of the Find and Replace dialog box.

The Find tab of the Find and Replace dialog box.

6. Make sure that the Find What box is empty and that the insertion point is in it.
7. Press **Ctrl+B**. Word indicates that you want to find bold text.
8. Select the Highlight All Items Found check box.
9. Click Find All. Word highlights all the words in the document that are bold.
10. Press **Ctrl+C**. All the words are copied to the Clipboard.
11. Switch to the blank document.
12. Press **Ctrl+V**. All the words are now in the previously blank document, one word per line.

With the words in their own document, you can easily sort them and look for any duplicates. Get rid of the duplicates so that you have a list of unique words and phrases, one per line. You then need to convert the words to a table; just select them, display the Insert tab of the ribbon, and choose Tables | Convert Text to Table. What you should end up with is a table that has a single column with your words and phrases in that column. (If you end up with multiple columns, you may want undo the conversion and look for any Tab characters in the list of words and phrases. If you find them, delete them, as they trigger the conversion to add another column.)

With all your words and phrases in a single column, add a second column just to the right of the first one. For the AutoMark feature to work best, the first column needs to contain the words or phrases you want marked in the document and the second column needs to contain how you want those words and phrases to appear in the index.

For instance, you might have multiple variations of the same phrase in the first column, such as "tallied results," "tally results," "tallied responses," and "tally responses." If you want each of these to appear in the index under the phrase "tallying results," then you would place that phrase to the right of each of the original phrases. If you want the word or phrase in the left column to be the same word or phrase used in the index, then just copy it from the left column to the right column.

When you are done with your list, save the document. You can then use what you've created to AutoMark the original document, in this manner:

1. Display the References tab of the ribbon.
2. Click the Insert Index tool. Word displays the Index tab of the Index dialog box.

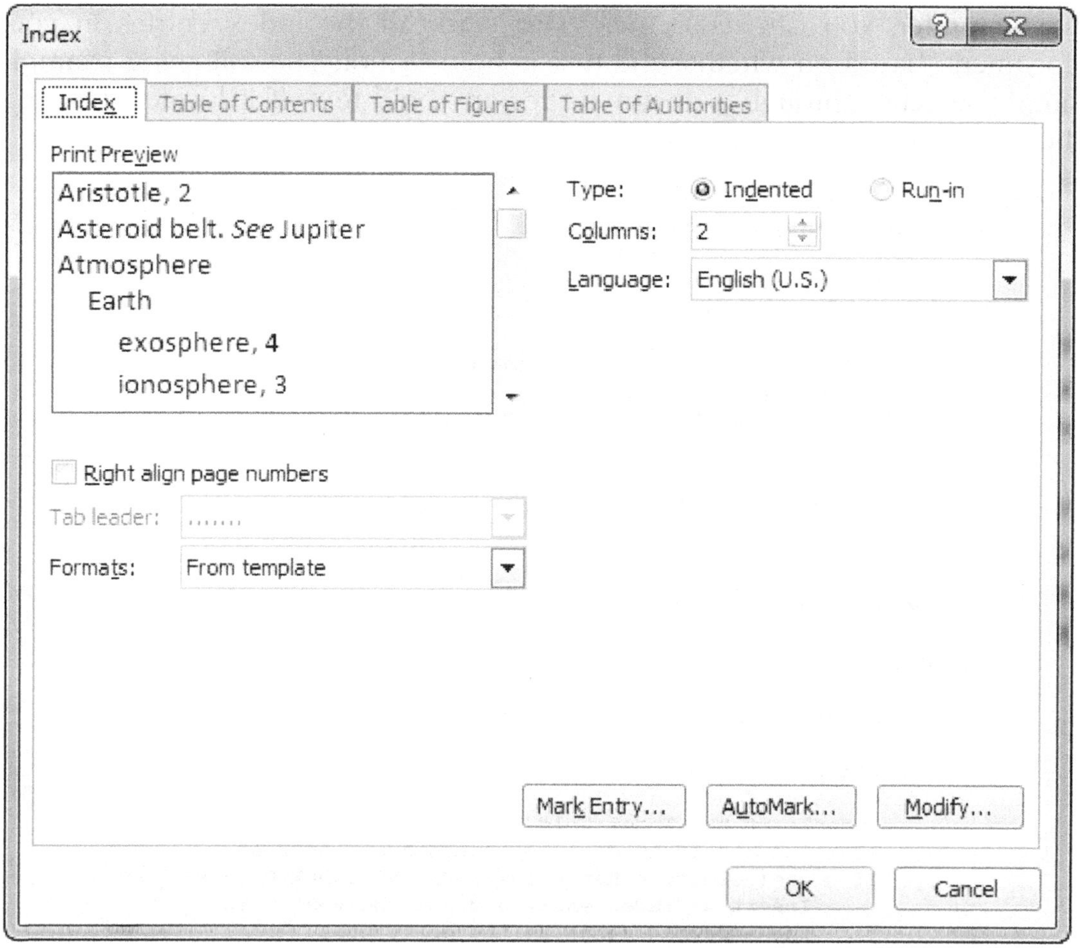

The Index tab of the Index dialog box.

3. Click on the AutoMark button. Word displays the Open Index AutoMark File dialog box.
4. Use the controls in the dialog box to select the file that contains your list of keywords and phrases.
5. Click Open.

That's it. Word uses your list of words as a "roadmap" to what it should mark in your document. When the AutoMark feature is done, you can then create your index as you desire.

If you prefer, you can use a macro to mark all the index entries in your document, based on whether the text is bold or not. The following example simply searches through a document for any bold text. If it locates that text, then it inserts an index entry there.

```
Sub InsertingIndexEntries()
    Application.ScreenUpdating = False

    'Go to the first page of the document
    Selection.HomeKey wdStory, wdMove

    'Set up the Find and Replace operation
    Selection.Find.ClearFormatting
    Selection.Find.Replacement.ClearFormatting
    With Selection.Find
        .Text = ""
        .Replacement.Text = ""
        .Forward = True
        .Wrap = wdFindContinue
        .Format = True
        .MatchWildcards = False
        .Font.Bold = True
    End With

    'Finds the bold text and inserts an index entry.
    Do
        Selection.Find.Execute
        If Selection.Find.Found Then
            'Checks if the Index field was selected
            'This occurs if it does not contain any entries
            If UCase(Selection.Range.Text) <> "NO INDEX ENTRIES FOUND." Then
                'Insert an index entry and use the text within
                'the selected range as the entry name
                ActiveDocument.Indexes.MarkEntry _
                  Range:=Selection.Range, _
                  Entry:=Selection.Range.Text, _
                  EntryAutoText:=Selection.Range.Text, _
                  CrossReference:="", _
                  CrossReferenceAutoText:="", _
                  BookmarkName:="", _
                  Bold:=False, _
                  Italic:=False, _
                  Reading:=""
                'Move past text that was found and the new index entry
                Selection.MoveRight wdCharacter, 1, wdExtend
                Selection.Collapse wdCollapseEnd
            End If
        End If
    Loop While Selection.Find.Found
```

```
    Application.ScreenUpdating = True
    Application.ScreenRefresh
End Sub
```

Remember that this macro finds any and all bold text in the document, including (possibly) places you may not expect. For instance, if you have some headings that are formatted as bold, those headings will be marked for the index, as well. Further, if you run the macro more than once, you may end up with multiple index entries for each bolded phrase or word. If you need to run it more than once, get rid of the existing index fields before you run it again.

Improper Index Page Numbers

Emily asked about a problem she was having with page references in indexes for a long document. It seems that when she inserted the index, some of the page numbers were off by one to three pages.

The first thing to check is your settings for hidden text in your document. When you insert index codes, they are inserted as fields with the hidden attribute applied to them. Word determines page counts based on what is visible on the screen, not necessarily on what is printed. Thus, you need to make sure that the display of hidden text is in sync with the printing of hidden text.

What happens if the settings aren't in sync? If hidden text is displayed (in other words, you can see the index entry codes, such as {XE "my indexed word"}), then the space taken by those visible codes are counted in the total page count. Over the course of a long document, this can affect pagination quite a bit. However, if Word is configured to not print hidden text, then the index page numbers—which are based on what is displayed, not what is printed—won't match the actual page numbers on the printout. (Remember that the display and the printing of hidden text are controlled independently of each other.)

The solution to this situation is fairly simple. All you need to do is follow these steps:

1. Click the File tab of the ribbon and then click Options. Word displays the Word Options dialog box.
2. At the left side of the dialog box click Display.

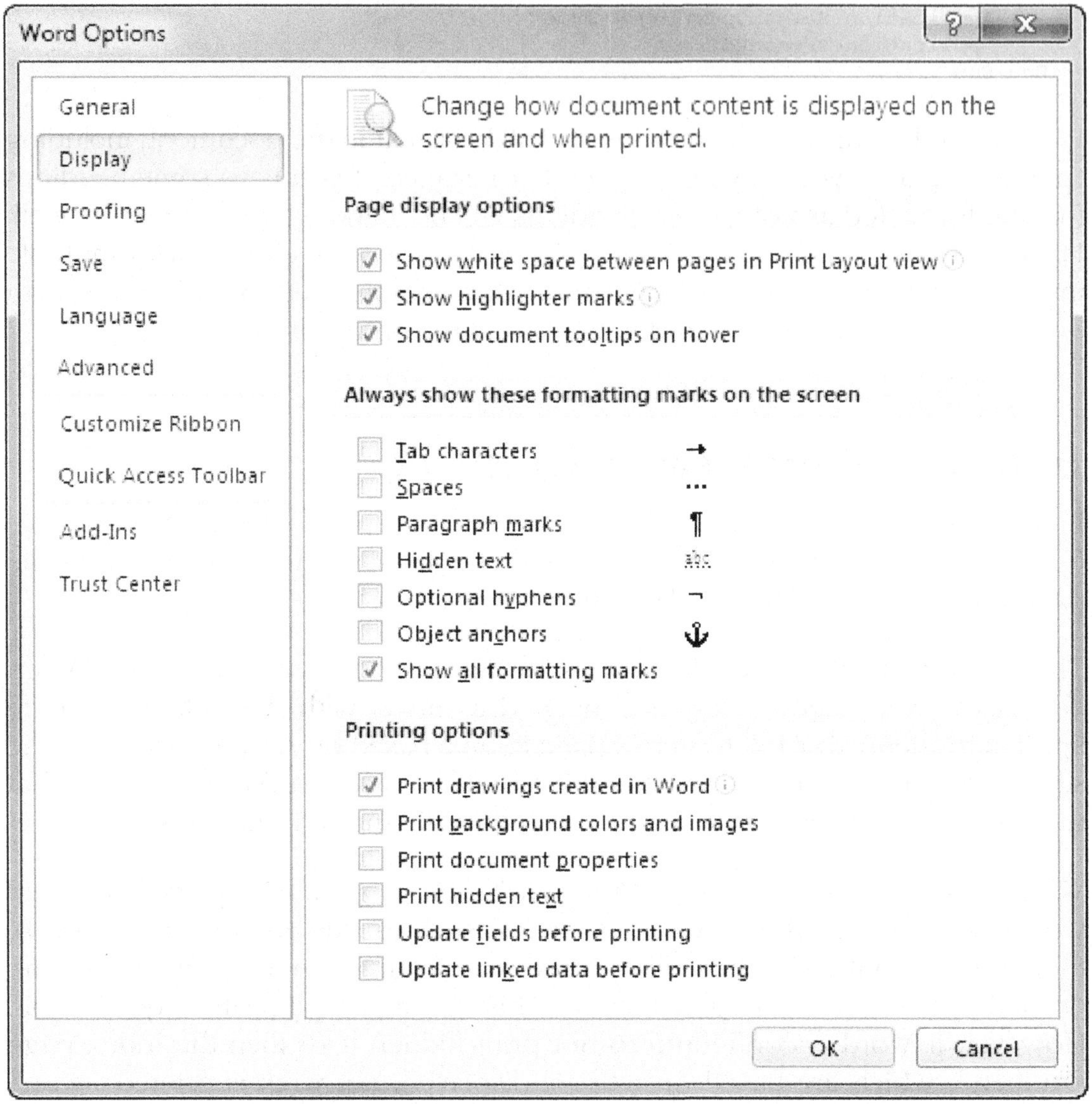

The Display options of the Word Options dialog box.

3. Make sure that both the Hidden Text and Show All Formatting Marks check boxes are cleared.
4. Scroll down a bit further in the dialog box and make sure the Print Hidden Text check box is selected.
5. Click OK.

6. Position the insertion point anywhere within the index.
7. Press **F9** to update the index.

Your index page numbers and your printing page numbers should now be in sync with each other. If they are not, then it could be that your document includes characters that, for whatever reason, can be displayed but cannot be printed. These would affect the displayed pagination—and thus the index page numbers—but not the printed pagination. You can discover if this is the case by carefully comparing your printout to what is displayed on your screen.

Finally, if these solutions still don't correct any page number disparities, it is possible that your document is corrupted in some way. This can occur in some documents, particularly documents that are used over the course of years and that had their roots in a different word processing program. You can try to open the file in WordPad and then use WordPad's Save As command to save the document back out. This will get rid of many of the advanced codes supported by Word by not by WordPad.

If the problem still persists, the only thing left to do is to get rid of all formatting and revert to plain text. Select all the text in the document (**Ctrl+A**), copy it (**Ctrl+C**), and paste it into a text editor such as Notepad. You can then copy it from within Notepad and paste it back into a new Word document. This process will get rid of any spurious formatting codes that may be corrupting the document. The only problem with such a drastic approach, of course, is that your document is now completely unformatted and you must reformat it and insert index codes all over again.

Specifying Index Section Dividers

You create an index by placing the special index field in your document. When you insert the field you can indicate how you want Word to separate the alphabetic sections of your index. There are several choices you can use, but you may need to experiment to find the dividers that are right for you. You specify these dividers by adding the \h switch to your index field. The following table shows some possible settings for this switch.

Switch	Meaning
\h " "	Sections are divided by a blank line.
\h "A"	Sections are divided by a single letter.
\h "----"	Sections are divided by four dashes (you can use more, if desired).
\h "text"	Sections are divided by whichever text you specify.
\h	Sections will have no divider; they will run together.

Specifying an Index Entry Separator

When you use an index field in your document you can indicate how you want Word to separate the index entry (or subentry) from the page number references or cross-references when it actually creates the index. This is done by adding the **\e** switch to your index field. You can use up to three characters for the separator, in the following manner:

```
\e "sep"
```

where ***sep*** represents the characters to use as the separator. For instance, if you use the following index field:

```
{index \e ": "}
```

Word, when compiling the index, will translate index entries to the following:

```
Widgets: 32, 38, 92
```

Notice that the index entry (**Widgets**) is separated from the page references by a colon and a space—exactly what was specified after the **\e** switch.

Specifying an Index Page-Range Separator

When you insert the index field in your document you can indicate how you want Word to separate page ranges in your index. Normally, Word uses a dash to separate the numbers in a range, as in the following example:

```
Widgets: 27-41
```

For some specialized indexes, you may want to use a different character other than a dash. You specify a different page range separator by adding the **\g** switch to your index field, followed by the character to use as a divider. For instance, the following field use specifies that a colon be used instead of a dash:

```
{index \g :}
```

Including Section Numbers in an Index

Word allows you to create dynamic indexes for your documents. These indexes can be generated, as needed, to reflect changes in page numbers within the document. The simplest of indexes contain only page numbers for the items being indexed. You may, however, want to create an index that also includes section numbers for entries.

There are two ways you can approach putting section numbers in an index. The easiest way is if the sections are just that—sections of your Word document, separated by section breaks. In this case, you can use compound fields so your index entries look something like this:

```
{XE "My Index Entry" \t "{SECTION}:{PAGE}"}
```

In this case you are using the \t switch to indicate that you want Word to substitute the text following the switch for the actual page number. Normally the \t switch is used for cross-references, but in this instance you are telling word to substitute the section number (generated by the SECTION field) followed by a colon and the page number (generated by the PAGE field). If you use this XE field to mark an index entry on page 6 of section 2, then the generated index will look like this:

```
My Index Entry. 2:6
```

The other method of including section numbers in your index comes in handy if your "sections" do not correspond to actual Word document sections. In this instance you use a different INDEX field to actually generate your index:

```
{INDEX \s MySection \d ":"}
```

The \s switch tells Word that you want the page numbers in the index to include the sequence number designated by the term following. In this instance, the entries in the index will include the number associated with the MySection sequence, followed by the character specified by the \d switch (a colon), and the page number. The sequence, of course, is set within the document by using the SEQ field:

```
{SEQ MySection}
```

Chapter Numbers in Indexes and TOAs

Pam wrote about a problem she was having with getting chapter-number prefixes to appear in her index and table of authorities. She could get the chapter number to appear in the table of contents, but not the other two elements.

Word is capable of using either of two general formats for page numbering: It can use either a number by itself, or it can use a combination of a prefix followed by a number. However, it can use only one page format in a given document. You set the format you want to use for a document by displaying the Insert tab of the ribbon, clicking the Page Number tool in the Header & Footer group, and then choosing Format Page Numbers. Word displays the Page Number Format dialog box.

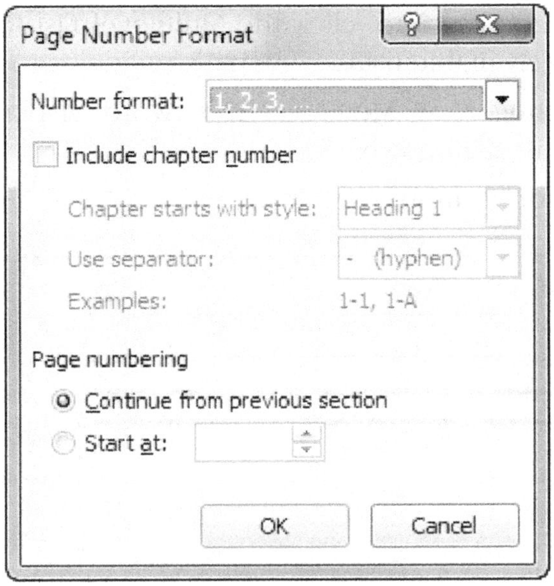

The Page Number Format dialog box.

Using the controls in the dialog box you can specify if Word is to include the chapter number with the page numbers it generates.

In order for chapter-number prefixes to work, the prefix must be a numbering format selected for one of the built-in heading styles that come with Word. This means that in order to include this prefix, your chapter heading style must be numbered. This would result in all chapters starting with a number, which is generally not the way chapters start. To prevent this, the number that Word adds to the chapter heading must be formatted as hidden.

The general steps, then, are to first use a Heading style for your chapter name and number. Then, number the chapter headings using hidden text, pick a page format that will use heading numbers, and then create your indices, table of contents, table of authorities, etc. The steps are:

1. Format your chapter headings as, say, Heading 1. If you have one chapter per document, then you will need to do this (and all these steps) in each document.
2. Place the insertion point in the heading and display the Home tab of the ribbon.

3. In the Paragraph group, click the Multilevel List tool. Word displays a selection of available lists.
4. Choose Define New Multilevel List. Word displays the Define New Multilevel List dialog box.
5. Click the More button.

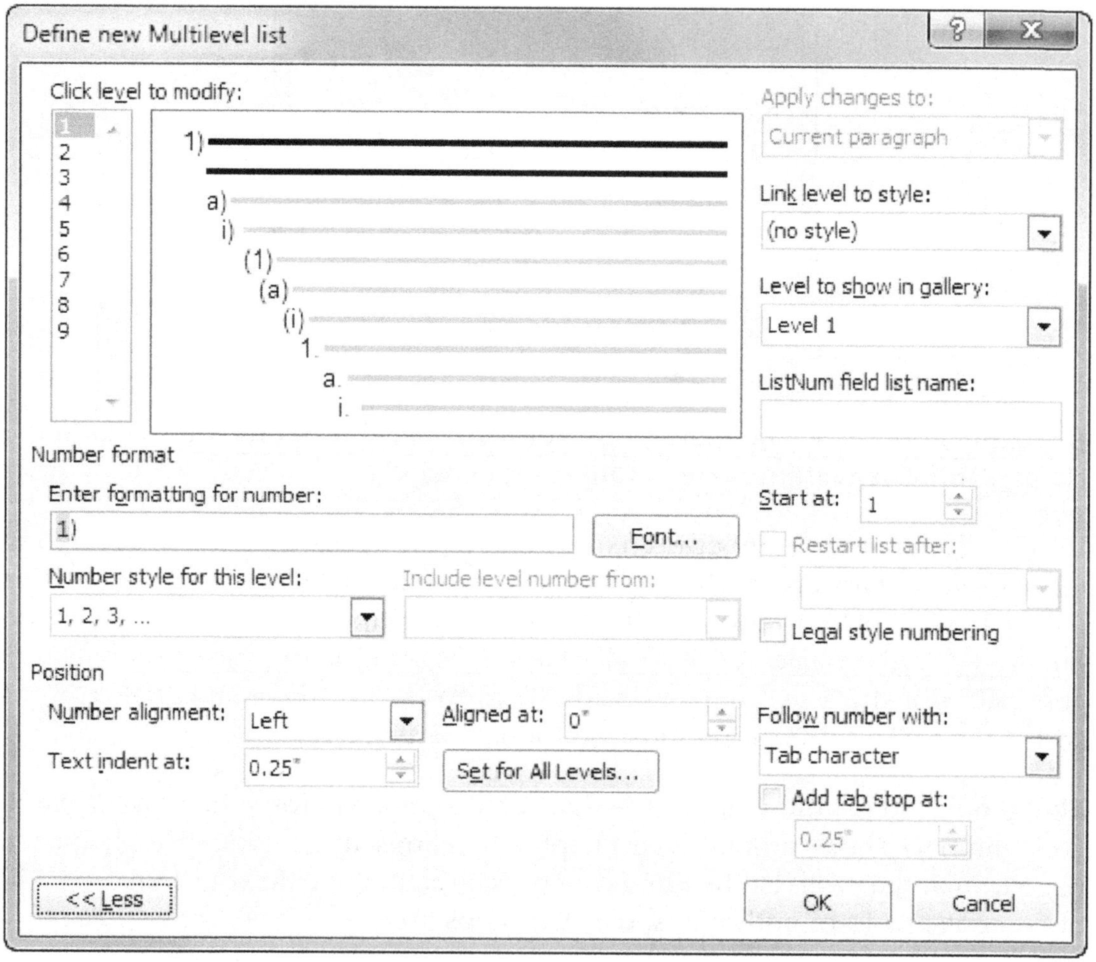

The Define New Multilevel List dialog box.

6. Change the Start At value to be the same as the chapter number. For instance, if you are working on the document for Chapter 5, then change the Start At value to 5.

7. Click the Font button. Word displays the Font dialog box. Notice that in the Formats area of the dialog box that all the controls are grayed out.

The Font dialog box.

8. Make sure the Hidden check box is selected (it has a bold check mark in it), then click on OK. The Font dialog box closes.

9. In the Customize Outline Numbered List dialog box, make sure that Number Alignment is set to Left and the Aligned At value is set to zero.

10. Click the More button. Word displays an expanded Customize Outline Numbered List dialog box.
11. Make sure the Link Level to Style drop-down list is set to Heading 1, and change the Follow Number With drop-down list to Nothing.
12. Click OK.
13. Display the Insert tab of the ribbon.
14. Clicking the Page Number tool in the Header & Footer group. Word displays a number of options.
15. Choosing Format Page Number. Word displays the Page Number Format dialog box.
16. Make sure the Include Chapter Number check box is selected.
17. Click on OK to dismiss the Page Number Format dialog box.

When you create your index or other special tables, the page numbers will show with the chapter-number prefixes in place. Because each chapter is a separate file, you must do this for each chapter, making sure to pick the appropriate start-at number in step 6.

4

Tables of Contents from Headings

Creating a Table of Contents from Heading Levels

If you are writing a long document or a book, you may want to create a table of contents (TOC) for your document. An easy way to create a TOC is to use heading levels, as defined by the Word styles. To do this, follow these steps:

1. Position the insertion point where you want the TOC inserted.
2. Display the References tab of the ribbon.
3. Click Table of Contents in the Table of Contents group. Word displays a drop-down list of TOC options.
4. Choose Insert Table of Contents. Word displays the Table of Contents tab of the Table of Contents dialog box.

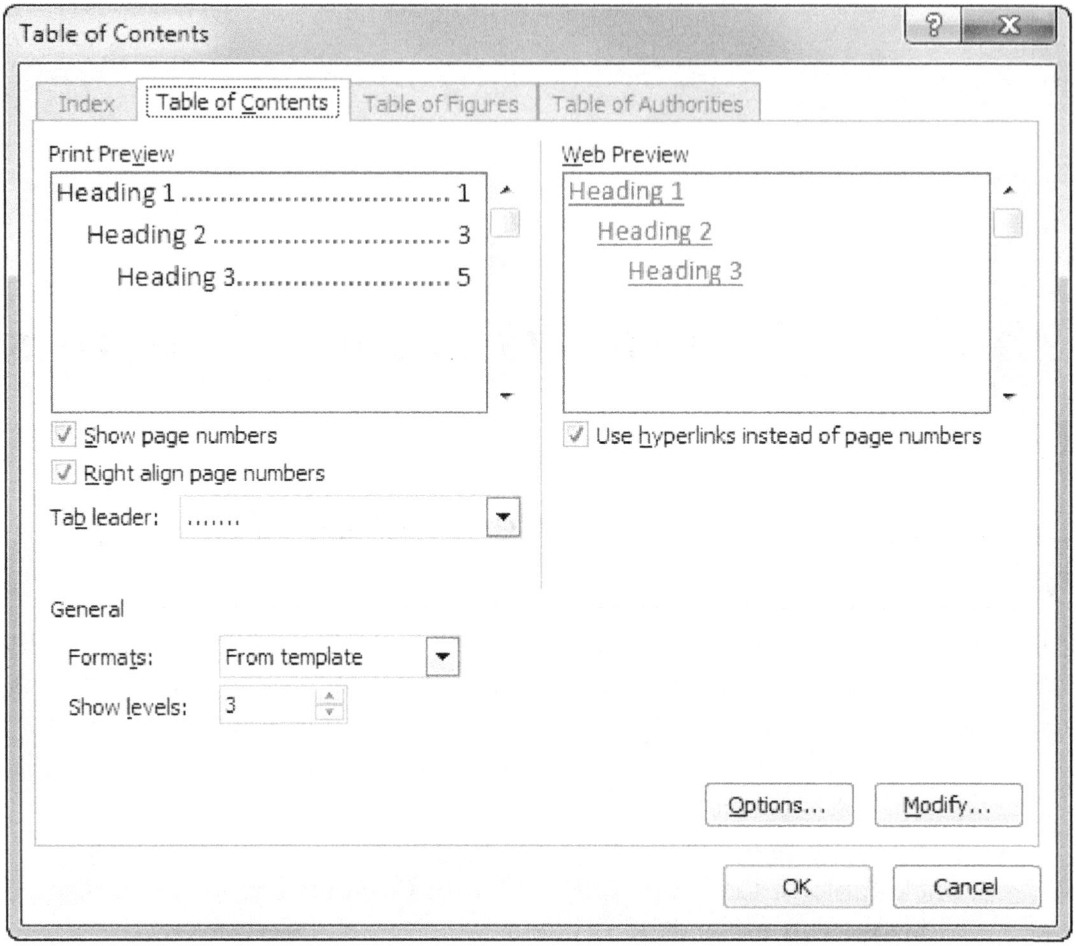

The Table of Contents tab of the Table of Contents dialog box.

5. Make sure that the Formats drop-down list is set to From Template.
6. Click on OK.

Controlling the Number of Heading Levels in a TOC

When you create a table of contents for your document, Word normally includes three heading levels in the TOC. You are not limited to three heading levels, however. You can adjust the number of heading levels that will be in a new TOC by following these steps:

1. Position the insertion point at the location in the document where you want the table of contents.
2. Display the References tab of the ribbon.
3. At the left of the ribbon click the Table of Contents tool. Word displays a few options.
4. Click Insert Table of Contents. Word displays the Table of Contents dialog box.

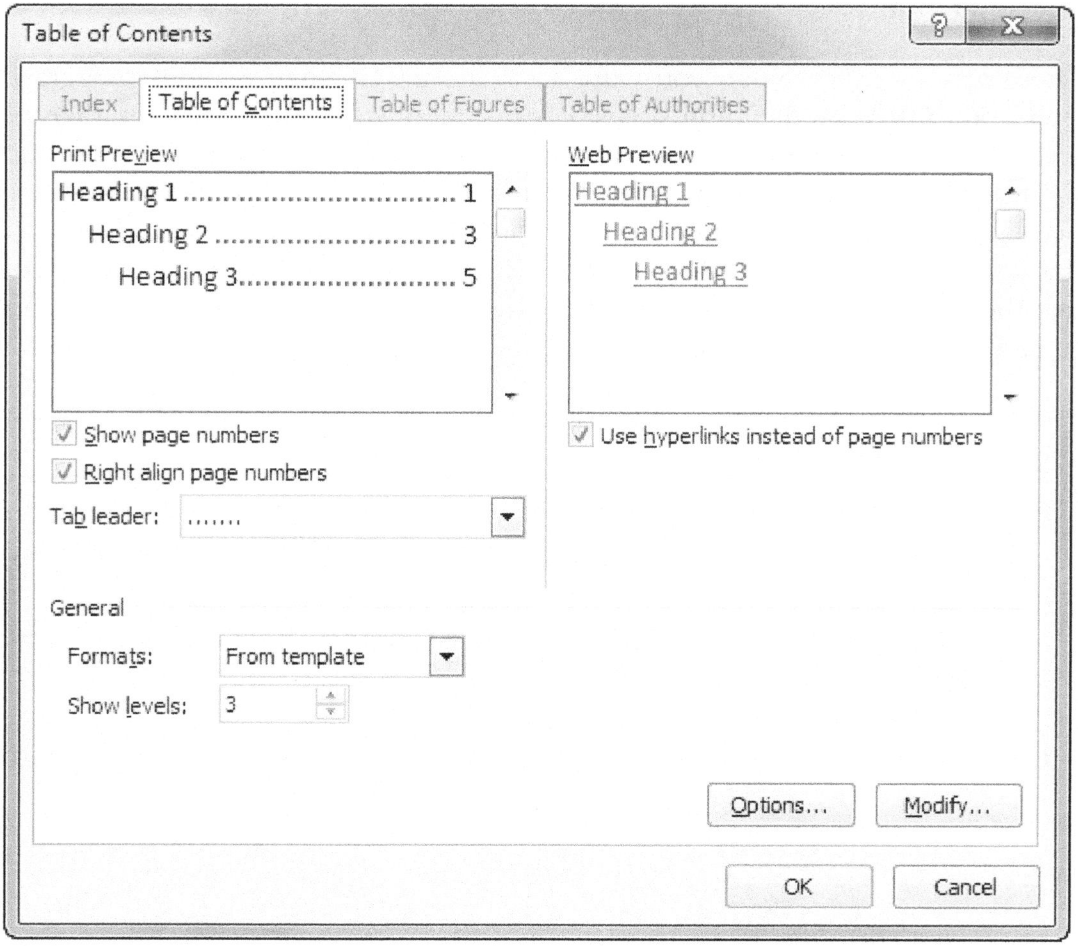

The Table of Contents tab of the Table of Contents dialog box.

5. Using the Show Levels control, indicate how many levels of headings you want to appear in the TOC.
6. Click on OK to close the Table of Contents dialog box and generate the table of contents.

Creating a TOC that Includes Specific Styles

The normal way to create a table of contents (TOC) is to let Word automatically create one based upon the headings in a document. Each paragraph formatted with the Heading 1 style, Heading 2 style, and Heading 3 style are automatically pulled into the TOC.

There may be times when you want to create a TOC that includes paragraph styles other than the heading styles. For instance, you might have a paragraph style you've created for a specific purpose, such as for denoting all the product names in a document. You don't want to format these product names as headings; you instead want to format them with a special paragraph format that calls them out in some manner specific to your needs. (Let's say that you use the style named SpecialProduct for this purpose.) If you then, later, want to include those product names in a special TOC, you can follow these steps:

1. Position the insertion point at the location in the document where you want the table of contents.
2. Display the References tab of the ribbon.
3. At the left of the ribbon click the Table of Contents tool. Word displays a few options.
4. Click Insert Table of Contents. Word displays the Table of Contents dialog box.

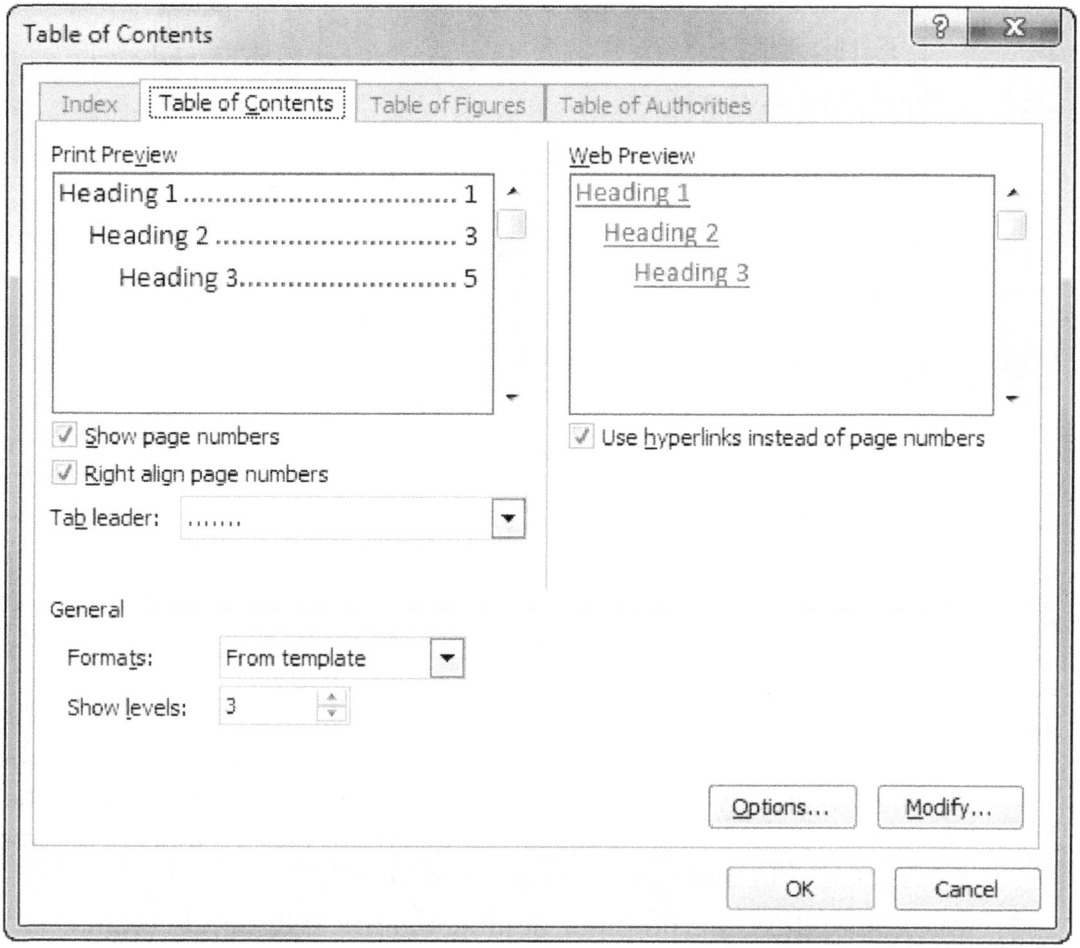

The Table of Contents tab of the Table of Contents dialog box.

5. Click on the Options button. Word displays the Table of Contents Options dialog box.

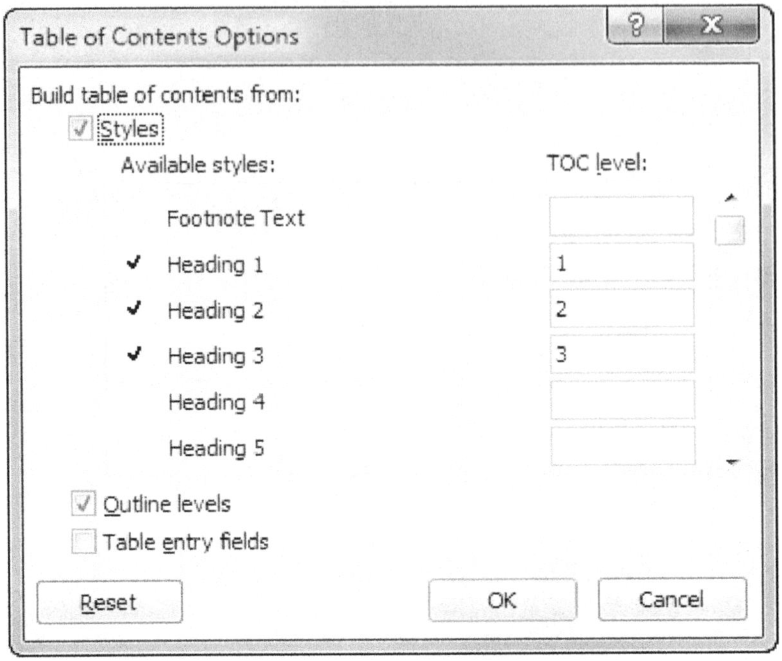

The Table of Contents Options dialog box.

6. Change the TOC Level column so that a 4 appears next to the SpecialProduct style. This indicates that you want any paragraphs that are formatted using the SpecialProduct style to end up in the TOC and be formatted in that table with the TOC 4 style.
7. Make sure there are no other numbers in the TOC Level column.
8. Click on OK to close the Table of Contents Options dialog box.
9. Click on OK to close the Table of Contents dialog box and generate the table of contents.

The result of creating this TOC in this way is that you have a list of all your products, and they are formatted in the list using the TOC 4 style. You can modify the TOC 4 style to reflect how you want the products to appear in the TOC.

You'll note that these steps used TOC level 4 (the TOC 4 style) for the products. The reason for this is simple—it allows you to leave TOC levels 1 through 3 (the TOC 1, TOC 2, and TOC 3 styles) for use in the regular TOC for the document. That way you can use different formatting for the regular TOC and the special product list TOC.

Problems with TOC Styles

Word allows you to quickly and easily create a table of contents, based upon the headings in your document. Exactly how you do this has been covered elsewhere in this e-book, but suffice it to say that you can generate a TOC based upon any headings that are formatted using Word's built-in heading styles—Heading 1, Heading 2, etc. (You can specify differently named styles to be used when generating the TOC, but that is beyond the scope of this particular tip.)

When the TOC is generated, the styles applied to the TOC entries are TOC 1, TOC 2, etc. There is typically a direct correspondence between the TOC style name and the heading style name. Thus, TOC 1 is used to format the TOC entry generated from a Heading 1 paragraph. Likewise, TOC 2 is used to format a TOC entry generated from a Heading 2 paragraph, and so on.

The bottom line is that if you want to change the way your TOC looks, all you need to do is define the attributes that make up the TOC styles (TOC 1, TOC 2, etc.). There is one very, very large caveat to this general statement, however: If you have applied explicit formatting to your headings, then your TOC will not look as you expect it to.

For instance, let's say that you define the TOC 1 style so it is 14-point Arial in black type. However, you may have used explicit formatting on a Heading 1 paragraph so that it is red, 16-point type. When you generate your TOC, the explicit formatting you applied affects what appears in your actual TOC. The result is that your TOC entry shows up as red, 16-point text, even though the TOC 1 style doesn't call for that. You can change the TOC styles after generating the TOC, but when you later regenerate, the TOC will again appear messed up.

The only solution to this problem is to make sure that none of your headings use explicit formatting; they should rely only on styles. Select each heading in your document and press **Ctrl+Q** (to return the text to the default paragraph settings for the style) and **Ctrl+Space Bar** (to return the text to the default font settings for the style). If, after doing this, you don't like the way your headings look, make the changes in the heading styles, not in the headings themselves. Then, when you later generate a TOC, you will get what you want—a TOC that matches the specifications in the TOC styles.

A similar problem often occurs in the course of developing the headings in a document. Let's say that you add a few headings, and you put them in all caps. (After all, you decided up front that you want your headings in all caps.) Then, you discover that you can set the format of the heading styles to be all caps. Now, you can type as you normally would, but Word displays the headings as all caps—just as you want.

When it comes time to create your TOC, Word pulls the text from the headings, and you discover that your TOC entries look terrible. Some Toc Entries Look Like This, OTHERS LIKE THIS, and still others like this. While the headings all appear in upper case within the body of the document, the text within those headings is inconsistent and the inconsistency is apparent when you generate the TOC.

The only way around this problem is to go back and re-enter your headings using the proper case. Normally, this will be what is called Title Case, which means that major words within the heading are capitalized, but other words are not. When the headings are consistently entered, what you see when you generate a TOC will not be a surprise.

5

Tables of Contents from Fields

Specifying a Table of Contents Entry

If you are creating a regular table of contents from headings within the document, you don't need the information in this tip. Instead, you should refer to the TOC tips provided elsewhere in this e-book. If you are creating a specialized TOC, however, then you will need the information in this tip. Examples of a specialized TOC would be a table of figures, illustrations, or tables. To create these types of TOCs, you must follow these two basic steps:

1. Specify what you want in the TOC.
2. Generate the TOC.

The first step is done by the following these steps; the second is covered in the next tip.

1. Position the insertion point immediately after the text you want included in the TOC.
2. Press **CTRL+F9** to insert a set of field braces. Make sure the insertion point stays between the braces.
3. Type **tc**, followed by the TOC entry within quotes. Thus, if you want the entry to be "North American Mammals", enter **tc "North American Mammals"** between the field braces.
4. Repeat steps 1 through 3 for each TOC entry you want to define.

Creating a Table of Contents from TOC Fields

Word allows you to create a table of contents using your own TOC specifications. You do this by first inserting TOC fields in your document (as described in the previous tip) and then compiling the actual TOC. To compile the TOC, follow these steps:

1. Position the insertion point at the location in the document where you want the table of contents.
2. Display the References tab of the ribbon.
3. At the left of the ribbon click the Table of Contents tool. Word displays a few options.
4. Click Insert Table of Contents. Word displays the Table of Contents dialog box.

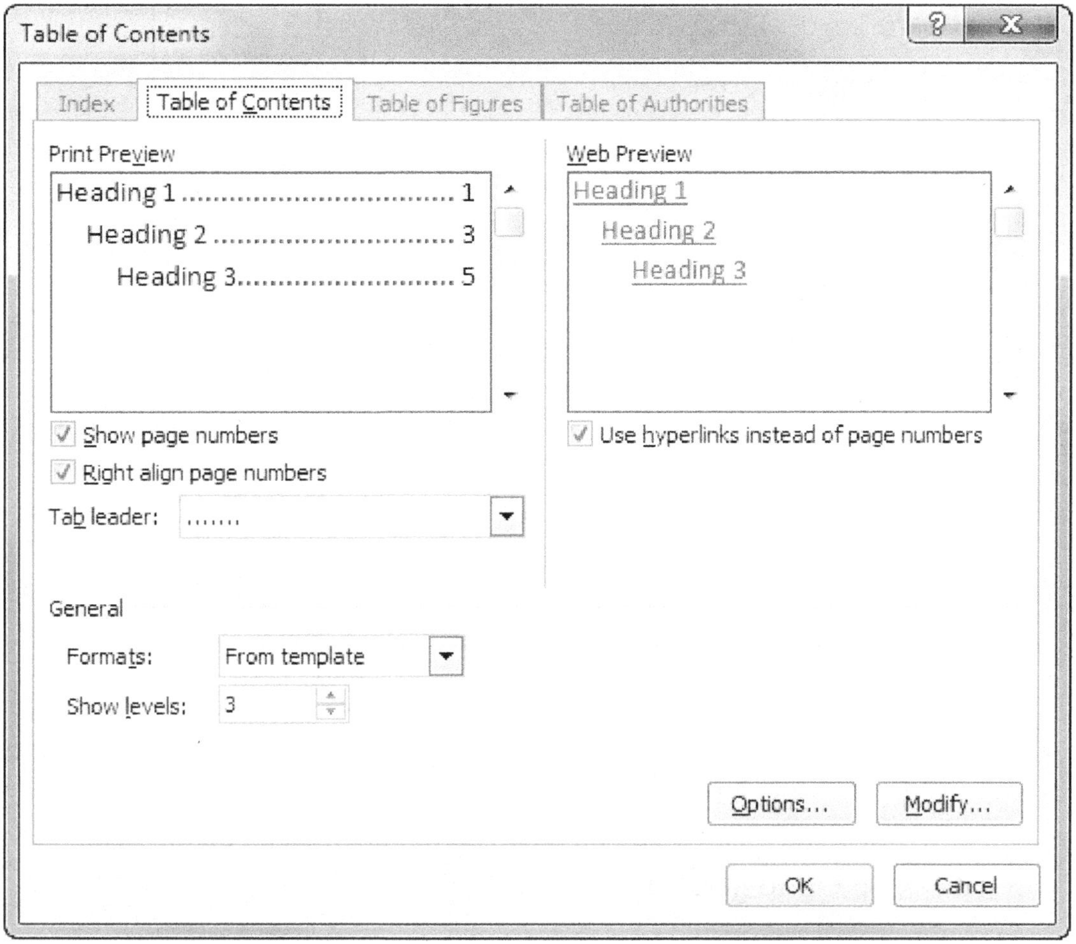

The Table of Contents tab of the Table of Contents dialog box.

5. Click on the Options button. Word displays the Table of Contents Options dialog box.

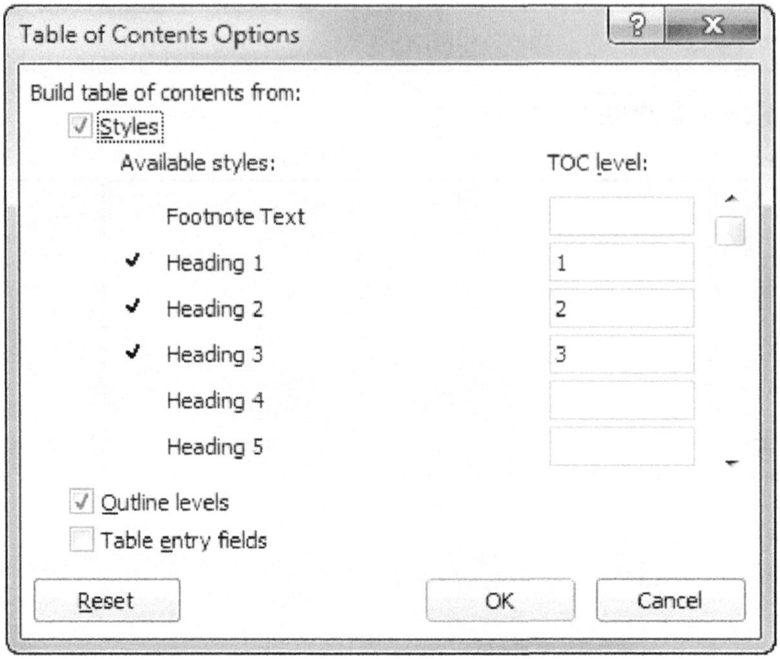

The Table of Contents Options dialog box.

6. Make sure the Table Entry Fields check box is selected (at the bottom of the dialog box).
7. Click on OK to close the Table of Contents Options dialog box.
8. Click on OK to generate your TOC.

Two-Line Headings in a TOC

Nilda generates tables of contents all the time in Word. She uses the Mark Entry feature to mark what should go in each table of contents. There are times when she may have a section title that consists of two lines separated by a hard return. When she marks the title as a single TOC entry, it doesn't appear in the generated TOC, and Nilda wonders why this is the case.

The reason is intrinsic to how Word puts together its TOCs. While a TC field (used to mark TOC entries) can presumably include a paragraph break, Word ignores everything after that break when it composes the TOC from those fields.

The solution is to get rid of the paragraph break. You have two options. First, you could edit your TC field contents so that the paragraph break is not included in the field. Second, you could actually modify your document so that the two lines of your heading are separated by a soft return (**SHIFT+ENTER**) instead of a hard return (**ENTER**).

If you choose the second route, then when Word compiles the TOC it will include the entire heading as a single entity, automatically replacing the soft return with a space.

A good place to find some great ideas on TOCs in Word is at this page, created by Word MVP Suzanne Barnhill:

```
http://sbarnhill.mvps.org/WordFAQs/TOCTips.htm
```

Using TC Fields for Notes

There are many times you may need to keep a "list" of editing work that needs to be done on a document. Keeping such a list manually, particularly in regards to a long document, can be difficult. Usually I put some sort of textual key in the document for which I can later search to find the location of where work needs to be done. For instance, I may put the text *****HERE** in the document, knowing that I can search for that and find the exact spot that needs work.

There is another approach that can be taken, however. This involves the use of the TC field, which is normally used to mark table of contents entries. You can also use these fields to indicate places where work needs to be done. This works because you can place anything within the TC field, and what you enter ends up in the TOC. This makes them a natural for creating notes to yourself. For example, you could use any of the following TC fields within your document:

```
{tc "send this tc tip to Allen Wyatt for WordTips"}
{tc "check this formula for accuracy"}
{tc "rewrite this paragraph before it leaves your desk"}
```

The potential uses are virtually endless. Later, when you are ready to do your editing work, you simply generate a TOC at the beginning of your document.

The entries dutifully end up there, and since the page numbers are hyperlinks, double-clicking the page numbers will take you to the spot where you need to work.

6

Table of Contents Gallery

Inserting a Preformatted Table of Contents

If you have a relatively simple document for which you want a table of contents, Word makes it easy to create one. The program provides, by default, three predefined styles you can use. You can see these TOC styles in what is called the "Table of Contents Gallery." Follow these steps:

1. Position the insertion point at the location in the document where you want the table.
2. Display the References tab of the ribbon.
3. At the left of the ribbon click the Table of Contents tool.

That's it. At the top of the options presented you can see the options available in the gallery. As mentioned, there are three styles already in the gallery, by default. These are:

- **Automatic Table 1.** Word creates a TOC based on the first three heading levels in your document. These levels are analogous with the styles Heading 1, Heading 2, and Heading 3. Anything formatted with those styles ends up in the TOC.
- **Automatic Table 2.** Same as Automatic Table 1, but with a slightly different appearance. (Wording at the top of the created table is different, as are the font attributes used in the table.)
- **Manual Table.** Word simply creates the shell for the TOC, and then

you manually type what makes up the table. This TOC is not updated automatically as you change the contents of your document.

The preformatted styles in the gallery are great if you have a need to create a simple table of contents. If you need more control over how your table of contents looks or what it includes, you will want to create your own table of contents using information in other tips in this e-book.

Adding a TOC to the Table of Contents Gallery

You can spend quite a bit of time creating a table of contents, getting it to look exactly as you want it to appear. If you want to use that table of contents—the way it appears—in other documents, you might consider adding it to the table of contents gallery. To do this, follow these general steps:

1. Create your table of contents, as desired.
2. Select the entire table of contents. Make sure you include not just the TOC itself, but any headings that should appear before the TOC.
3. Display the References tab of the ribbon.
4. At the left side of the ribbon click the Table of Contents tool. A series of choices appear.
5. Click Save Selection to Table of Contents Gallery. Word displays the Create New Building Block dialog box.

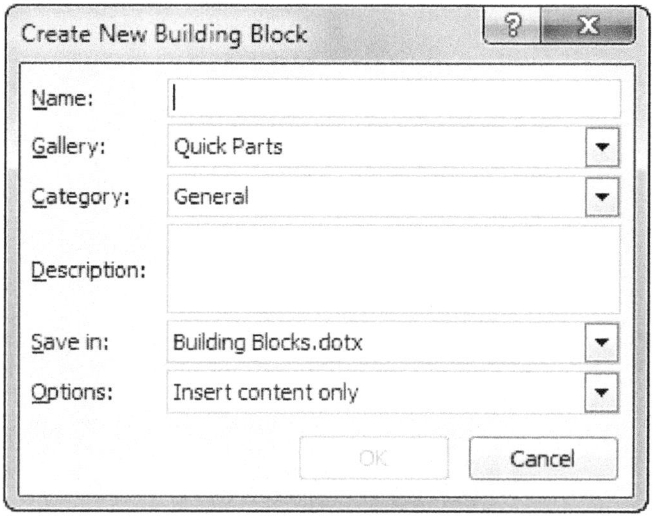

The Create New Building Block dialog box.

6. Change the contents of the Name field to reflect the name you want used for this particular table of contents.
7. Click OK.

As you can probably tell, new entries in the table of contents gallery are considered building blocks. They are the same, in many respects, to other building blocks you may create in your document. Because they are placed in the Table of Contents gallery (see the Create New Building Block dialog box), they will appear as predefined options when you later want to insert a TOC in your document. Choose the gallery option, and the table of contents you defined appears in the document at the insertion point.

7

Formatting a Table of Contents

Creating a TOC without Hyperlinks

Word is currently a "well connected" program, meaning that it handles—many times automatically—hyperlinks and other accoutrements of our connected computing society. It didn't always used to be that way. In fact, Web-related features were added to Word incrementally, over a number of versions.

One manifestation of this was a change made to how Word creates tables of contents—they include hyperlinks for each TOC entry, so that when you click on them, you jump directly to the corresponding head in the document.

What if you don't want hyperlinks in your TOC, however? Unfortunately, there is no check box or configuration setting you can use to turn off this behavior. Instead, you must follow these steps to get rid of the hyperlinks:

1. Position your insertion point somewhere within your TOC.
2. Press **Shift+F9**. The TOC disappears and the underlying field code is displayed in its stead. The field code should look something like this:

   ```
   { TOC \o "1-3" \n \h \z }
   ```

   The actual appearance of the field code will differ, based on how you asked the TOC to be constructed.
3. Remove the \h switch. This is the switch that causes Word to treat the TOC entries as hyperlinks.

4. Press **F9**. Word displays the Update Table of Contents dialog box.
5. Make sure the Update Entire Table radio button is selected.
6. Click on OK.

You should note that you will need to follow these steps each time you use Word to insert your TOC. The exception to this is if you create your own table of contents gallery entry (a building block), as discussed elsewhere in this e-book.

Adding Column Headings to a Table of Contents

Vincent has a table of contents that spans multiple pages. At the beginning of the TOC he inserted headings for each of the columns (i.e., Section, Page, etc.). He wants to get these column headings to appear on the ensuing pages, as well.

The problem here is that a table of Contents, in Word, is a table in name only—it is actually the result of a field and not a real table. That being said, there are a few approaches you can take to display your desired headings on each page.

One approach is to convert the field results (the table of contents) to regular text by selecting the TOC and pressing **Ctrl+Shift+F9**. Once done, you can then convert the text to a real Word table and add your repeating headings as you normally would in any other table. The drawback to this approach, of course, is that the table of contents is no longer dynamic. If edits to your document necessitate a change in the TOC, you will need to make that change manually.

Another approach is to insert continuous section breaks both before and after the TOC. In the section containing the TOC (and only in that section) modify the page header so that it contains the TOC headings. This page header will be repeated for each page on which the TOC appears. This approach will take some tweaking, however, to get the page header to be close enough to where the TOC starts at the top of each page.

A third (and perhaps easiest) approach is to create a table that consists of two rows and one column. Format the table so that it does not have any borders. In the first row of the table place the headings that you want repeated at the top of each page of the TOC. In the second row of the table place your actual TOC. Format the first row of the table (the one with your headings) as you would any table row that you want to repeat.

Creating an Inline Heading

Pete notes that APA style defines a level-three heading as being indented in italic on the same line as the first sentence in the paragraph. ("APA style" means the style guide devised and published by the American Psychological Association. You can find more information at http://www.apastyle.org.) Pete's question is how to define an inline heading style that will appear properly in the table of contents without including the rest of the paragraph in the TOC.

There are two common ways of approaching this problem. First, you can simply create your level-three heading and body text as you normally would, each in their own paragraph. Then, select the paragraph mark at the end of the heading (you may need to configure Word to display paragraph marks) and format the paragraph mark as hidden text. As long as your copy of Word is not configured to print hidden text, your heading will appear inline with your body text, and the TOC will appear just as you expect.

The second option is to use what is called a "style separator." It basically allows a selection of text to have a paragraph style applied to it. The easiest way to use this type of formatting is to type your heading text followed by your body text, in a single paragraph. Make sure the entire paragraph is formatted as body text, then select just the text that will comprise the heading. Apply the level-three heading style to this selected text. The selected text now has your heading formatting and the rest of the paragraph is formatted as body text.

When you format in this manner, Word generates the proper TOC, as you would expect. What it doesn't do well is apply any paragraph features that are different than the paragraph features in your body text format. So, for instance, if your level-three heading is formatted to include a half-inch indent from the left margin, that indent will not be applied to the selected text. Instead, the paragraph attributes of the body text format will be used.

Word also includes an internal command called InsertStyleSeparator, which can be added to the Quick Access Toolbar. This tool allows you to "separate" text so that two paragraph styles are applied to what appears to be a single paragraph. In reality this tool does nothing more than what has already been described. The command is described in this Knowledge Base article:

`http://support.microsoft.com/?kbid=285059`

Basically you format your heading using your level-three heading style, use the InsertStyleSeparator command to indicate you want to start a new style, type the rest of the paragraph, and apply the body text style to the rest of the paragraph. The inserted "style separator" keeps the application of the body text style from affecting the application of the heading style before the separator.

For a great write-up of different ways you can set up inline headings, see this page by Word MVP Suzanne Barnhill:

`http://sbarnhill.mvps.org/WordFAQs/RunInSidehead.htm`

Customized Tables of Contents

Have you ever created a table of contents for a document? Word makes it easy to do, as described elsewhere in this e-book. What if you want to customize the way in which the tables are formatted by Word?

For most formatting of TOCs, all you need to do is change the various styles assigned to the TOC entries by Word. For a standard table of contents, the style TOC 1 is used to format the TOC entry corresponding to paragraphs formatted with the Heading 1 style. Likewise, TOC 2 corresponds to Heading 2, TOC 3 to Heading 3, etc.

To change how the TOC entry looks, just change the formatting for the TOC styles. These styles are the same as any other paragraph style, so you can change font characteristics, alignment, indentation, spacing, borders, bullets—the works.

One way you might want to customize your TOC is to change a particular TOC entry so it doesn't show page numbers. A clever way to do this is to change the style for the TOC entry so that the page number prints to the right of the edge of your paper. Just adjust the tab stop defined in the appropriate TOC entry so it is at a setting such as 9 inches, which is outside the printing area of a normal sheet of paper.

The proper way to turn off page numbers for a particular TOC level is to use a switch in the field code used to create the TOC. For instance, if you wanted the TOC entries corresponding with Heading 2 paragraphs to not include page numbers, you could follow these steps:

1. Create your TOC as you normally would.
2. Position the insertion point somewhere inside the TOC.
3. Press **Shift+F9**. The entire TOC should collapse to a single field code, similar to what is shown here:

   ```
   { TOC \o "1-3" \h \z }
   ```

4. Modify the field code so it looks like this:

   ```
   { TOC \o "1-3" \n "2-2" \h \z }
   ```

5. With the insertion point still within the field, press **F9**. Word displays a dialog box that asks if you want to update the page numbers or the entire table.
6. Choose to update the entire table, then click OK.

The resulting TOC should show page numbers on all TOC entries, except those that use the TOC 2 style.

For a great article on using switches with TOC entries, see the following Web page:

`http://word.mvps.org/FAQs/Formatting/TOCSwitches.htm`

TOC Heading Numbers Always Show in Bold

Linda has a document that uses built-in heading styles that she's modified to use automatic numbering. When she generates a table of contents from these headings, the numbers and text are always bold. Linda thinks the table of contents looks better when it's not in bold text, so she modified the TOC styles so they weren't bold. However, Word still shows the numbers in the TOC (the automatic numbers, pulled from the headings, not the page numbers) in bold. Linda wonders how she can modify the TOC styles so that the numbers and the text are both not bold.

It is important to keep in mind that the problem may not necessarily be with the TOC styles. The problem could be with the headings in the document. When a TOC is generated, any explicit formatting in the headings is carried over to the TOC, as explicit formatting. Thus, if you have a heading for which the style is 14-point regular text, and someone selects the heading and changes the formatting (making it bold, changing the point size, etc.), then the explicit formatting is carried over to the TOC entry, overriding whatever the TOC style says should be used.

One way to test if this is the problem is to select a heading in your document (the entire paragraph, including the paragraph mark at the end of the paragraph) and press **Ctrl+Space Bar** then **Ctrl+Q**. The first shortcut returns the paragraph to the underlying character formatting as defined in the style and the second shortcut returns the paragraph to the underlying paragraph formatting defined in the style. If, after pressing these two shortcut keys, the heading looks different than it did before, then there was explicit formatting applied that would carry over and affect any TOC that relies on that heading. Your best bet at this point is to repeat this process with all the headings and then make any changes to the heading styles to reflect how you want the headings to really appear.

Because Word transfers explicit formatting from the headings to the TOC entries, this brings up something else you can do, if you'd like. You should be able to remove any explicit formatting from the TOC itself by selecting the entire

TOC and pressing **Ctrl+Space Bar** and **Ctrl+Q**. This works because, again, the explicit formatting (which was transferred by Word) is removed and the underlying TOC styles show through. The only problem with this approach is that you will need to redo it every time the TOC is regenerated, as the explicit formatting is retransferred every time the TOC is created.

8

Table of Contents Tricks

Page Ranges in a TOC

Colin asked if it is possible to construct a table of contents so it includes not just a starting page number, but a range of page numbers. For instance, the table of contents would include 1-1 to 1-22 instead of just 1-1.

Unfortunately, this is not possible in Word. The table of contents feature is designed to only include starting page numbers. It would appear that this decision is related to the fact that determining a starting page number is easy (it is the page on which the related heading starts), but an ending page number for a section is not as easily determined. Where a section ends depends on what headings you instruct Word to include in the TOC.

If you want page ranges in your TOC, the only way to get them is to manually enter the TOC and not rely on Word to create one automatically.

Two Types of Page Numbers in a TOC

Peggy generated a table of contents (TOC) that displayed correctly. Without warning the page number for the first entry in the TOC changed from "iii" to "3". (The page number that appears in the footer for that page is "iii".) Peggy didn't touch the TOC; it just changed and she can't get it to go back to "iii". She tried updating the TOC and it persists to display "3" in the TOC.

When compiling a table of contents, Word uses the same page number formatting as appears on the pages within the header or footer of each page. If the page number in the header or footer appears properly, then it should appear properly in the TOC.

You can verify this by selecting the entire document (press **Ctrl+A**) and updating all the fields in the document (press **F9**). In most documents both page numbers and tables of contents are implemented through the use of fields. When everything is updated, see if the page number appears properly in the TOC. If it doesn't, take a look at the page number that appears in the header or footer to see if it looks right.

If the page number looks wrong in the header or footer, then it is possible that a section break got deleted by mistake during routine editing. If the section break is still there, then it is possible that the page number format got messed up for the section that contains the page number. Either way, you will have some additional editing and formatting to do to get the situation straightened out.

If the page number looks OK in the header or footer, then it is possible that something is amiss with the styles used to display your TOC. You'll want to check the formatting specified for the styles to make sure that it is correct.

Using Multiple Tables of Contents

Word allows you to include multiple tables of contents in a single document. Thus, you can have a table of contents for each chapter of a book, even if all the chapters are in the same document.

In order to restrict the table entries for each separate table, you will have to use unique custom styles for each table. For example, you might use styles named "Chapter1Heading1", "Chapter1Heading2", and so on for the first chapter, and "Chapter2Heading1", etc., for the second chapter.

With your styles defined and applied to all the appropriate heads in your document, you are ready to generate the tables of contents. You can do this by following these steps:

1. Position the insertion point at the location in the document where you want the table of contents.
2. Display the References tab of the ribbon.
3. At the left of the ribbon click the Table of Contents tool. Word displays a few options.
4. Click Insert Table of Contents. Word displays the Table of Contents dialog box.

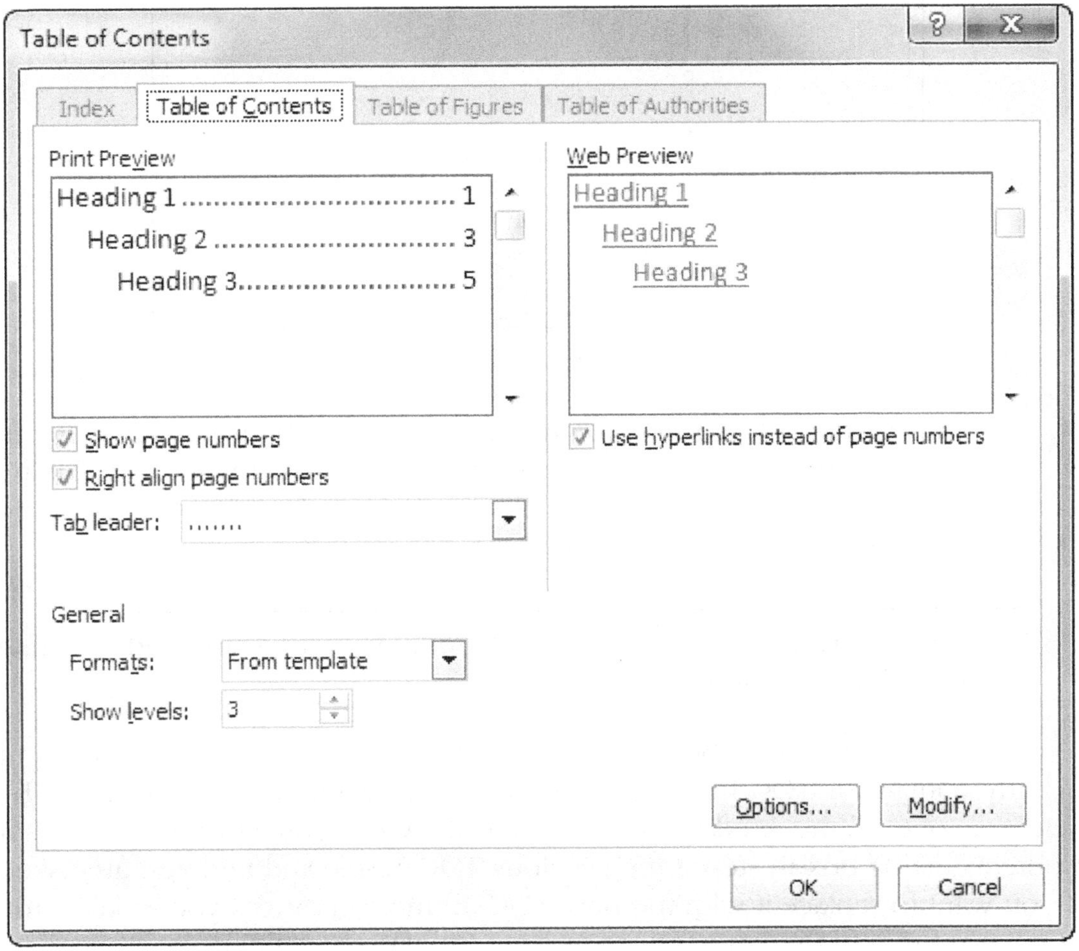

The Table of Contents tab of the Table of Contents dialog box.

5. Click on the Options button. Word displays the Table of Contents Options dialog box.

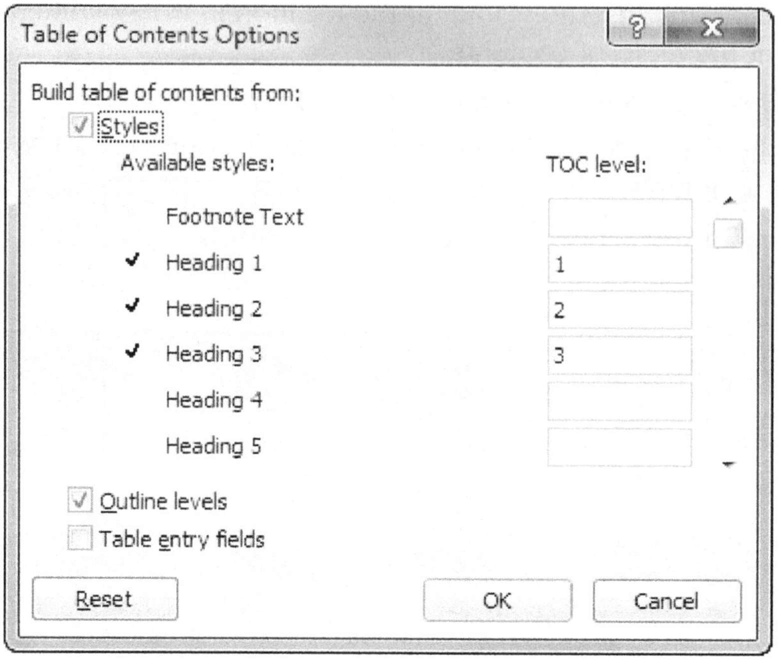

The Table of Contents Options dialog box.

6. Change the TOC Level column to reflect which styles you are using in the table of contents you are inserting. Thus, if you were using doing a TOC for Chapter 1, beside the "Chapter1Heading1" style you would place a 1 in the TOC Level column.
7. Click on OK to close the Table of Contents Options dialog box.
8. Click on OK to close the Table of Contents dialog box and generate the table of contents.

You should note that if, before following the above steps, your document already contains a TOC that was generated from a building block (done by selecting one of the predefined TOC styles), when you close the Table of Contents dialog box in step 8 the previous TOC is selected and you are asked if you want to replace it with the new TOC. In most instances you won't want; you'll want to add the new TOC to any you've already defined.

Insert a TOC without Upsetting Pagination

When you insert a table of contents in any version of Word, the table becomes part of the contents and forces the repagination of everything that follows. If you want your TOC to occupy its own page, that page will be numbered page 1, and your first section on page 2. Most of us prefer our first page of content to be listed as page 1.

One solution is to adjust the page numbering system to begin with page 0. Because page 0 is your TOC, your first content will begin on page 1. But if your TOC becomes longer than a page, this solution won't work.

There's an easier way: Before generating your table of contents, insert a new-page section break at the start of your first content. Then move to the newly created first section and generate your table of contents. It will list all the headings in your second section with the appropriate page numbers without affecting pagination. This tip also allows you to create a separate introductory section in Roman numerals, which will show its own numbering system in the TOC.

Generating a TOC that Includes Text Boxes

Some people love to use text boxes to help place text on their pages. In essence, the text boxes become elements of a larger page layout, used in order to get "just the right look." Unfortunately, using text boxes means making trade-offs in other areas. One of those areas is in relation to a table of contents.

A table of contents can be generated in two ways—using styles or using fields. (Details on this are covered elsewhere in this e-book.) If you generate your TOC using styles, and you have a heading style defined in a text box, Word still won't include it in the TOC. This is because text boxes are really graphics, and they are contained on a "graphics layer" or "drawing layer" in Word. Thus, text in a text box is a portion of the drawing layer and separate from the main text of your document.

If you generate your TOC using fields, then you rely on the placement of the TC field to designate a table of contents entry. Unfortunately, all the documentation available from Microsoft indicates that you cannot include certain fields in a text box—including TC fields.

If you must include the contents of your text boxes in a TOC, the only solution is to not use text boxes—you need to convert them to frames. In order to convert an existing text box to a frame, you follow these steps:

1. Right-click on the text box. Word displays a Context menu.
2. Choose the Format Text Box option from the Context menu. Word displays the Format Text Box dialog box.
3. Make sure that the Text Box tab is selected.
4. Click on the Convert to Frame button. Word asks if you are sure you want to convert.
5. Click on OK.

Locking Lines in a TOC

Charles described a situation in which his table of contents was working fine, except he wanted to jump to a heading when he pressed **Enter** with the insertion point at the beginning of the TOC entry that was hyperlinked.

When you automatically create a TOC in Word, the entries in the TOC are actively linked to the headings referenced by the TOC entry. This happens because Word uses the /h option with the TOC field, by default. If you hold down the **Ctrl** key as you click on a TOC entry, you are automatically taken to the appropriate heading.

The interesting thing is that if you position the insertion point anyplace within a TOC entry and press **Enter**, Word behaves as if you had used the mouse to activate the link and you are taken to the appropriate heading. Note that the insertion point must be inside the TOC entry, not just to the left of it. If the insertion point is at the beginning (or even at the very end, to the left of the paragraph mark), then pressing **Enter** will result in a new paragraph being inserted in the middle of the TOC.

This is apparently the way that Word is designed, and there is no way around this. You cannot "turn off" or modify the behavior of the ENTER key within a linked TOC. Nor can you "lock" the lines in a TOC so that ENTER doesn't insert new paragraphs if the insertion point is outside the actual TOC entry. The only thing you can do is remember to move the insertion point within the TOC entry—even by one character—before pressing ENTER.

Deleting a Table of Contents

At some point you may want to delete a table of contents that you previously placed in your document. Doing so is easy; all you need to do is make sure that you select the entire TOC and then press the DELETE key. Selecting the entire TOC is important. Since a TOC is generated from a field, if you don't select the entire TOC and delete it, then all you are doing is deleting a portion of the field results. In this case the underlying field remains intact, and the TOC reappears the next time the field is updated.

Another way to delete a TOC is to follow these steps:

1. Display the References tab of the ribbon.
2. At the left of the ribbon click the Table of Contents tool. A series of choices appear.
3. Click the Remove Table of Contents option

If the Remove Table of Contents option is not available (it is grayed out) then it means your document is either protected or it is open in compatibility mode. When you click the option the last-created TOC is removed from the document. (This is important to know in case you have multiple TOCs in the document; only the last TOC is deleted.)

If your table of contents was created from one of the defined table of contents gallery options, there is another way you can delete it. Simply click anywhere within the TOC and you will see a blue outline appear around the building block that makes up the TOC.

A TOC created from a building block is surrounded by a blue border.

Click the Table of Contents tool at the upper-left of the blue outline and you can then select Remove Table of Contents from the resulting choices.

Updating an Entire TOC from a Macro

If you have a document that contains a table of contents (TOC), and you update the fields in the entire document, Word asks if you want to update the entire table, the chapter entries, or just the page numbers associated with the existing chapter entries in the Table of Contents. This occurs because TOCs are implemented through the use of a field, and when you update all fields you are telling Word you also want to update the field underlying the TOC.

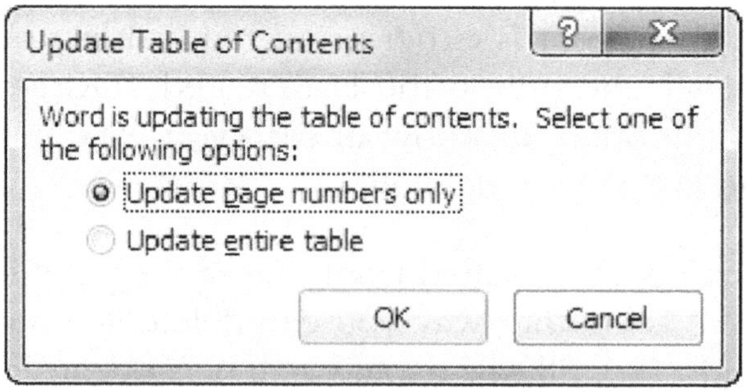

The Update Table of Contents dialog box.

You can update a TOC using a macro by utilizing the TablesOfContents collection. Each item in the collection represents a single TOC in the document. (In most documents the collection will consist of only a single item.) To update the entire TOC, you use this format of the command:

```
ActiveDocument.TablesOfContents(1).Update
```

The Update method is what does the work; it updates the TOC. If you want to update only the page numbers in the TOC, you use an entirely different method:

```
ActiveDocument.TablesOfContents(1).UpdatePageNumbers
```

Whenever you use commands like these in a macro, it is a good idea to make sure that there is actually a TOC in the document before you try to do any updating. The easiest way to do this is to just check the Count property for the collection, as shown here:

```
If ActiveDocument.TablesOfContents.Count = 1 Then _
  ActiveDocument.TablesOfContents(1).Update
```

9

Creating a Table of Authorities

Creating a Table of Authorities

In long legal documents, a table of authorities is often used to cite references to statutes, cases, and other sources for information referenced in the document. The table of authorities will cite the case or statute, along with the page number in the document on which the case or statute is referenced.

Word includes the ability to easily create a table of authorities. You do so by first marking citations within your document, and then instructing Word to compile the citations into your final table. As you are marking citations, you can specify both long and short versions of citations. For instance, a long citation may be something like "Smith v. Jones, 37 Adj. 3d 421 (1968)." The short version of the citation could be something like "Smith v. Jones" or even "Smith (1968)."

To mark citations, follow these steps:

1. Select the long, full citation you want to use.
2. Press **SHIFT+ALT+I**. Word displays the Mark Citation dialog box.

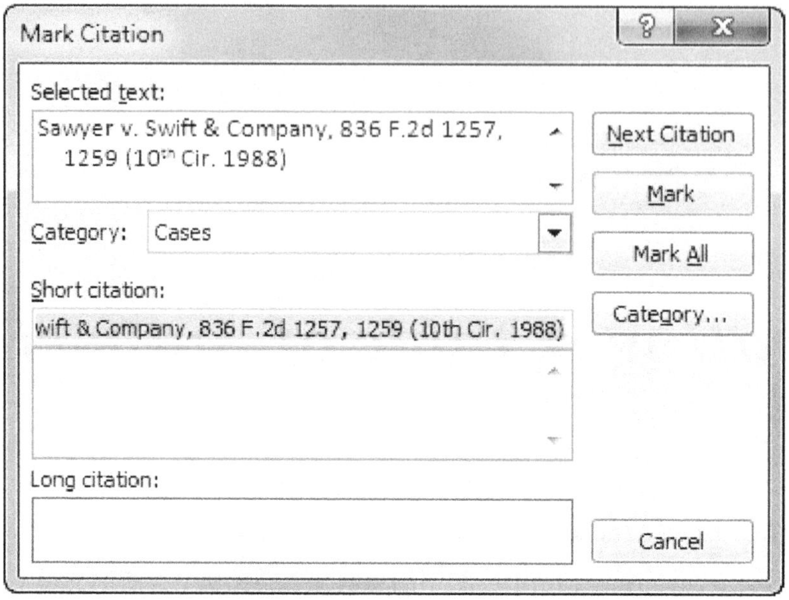

The Mark Citation dialog box.

3. Make any editorial changes desired to the text in the Selected Text box.
4. Using the drop-down Category list, select the category to which this citation belongs.
5. In the Short Citation box, edit the text to reflect the short version of the citation.
6. Click on Mark (to mark just the current, selected instance of the citation) or Mark All (to search the document and mark all instances).
7. Click on Cancel.

Generating a Table of Authorities

Adding a table of authorities to your document is a two-step process. First you need to mark all the citations within your document, and then you need to actually compile or generate the table. Once you have marked all the citations, you can generate the table of authorities by following these steps:

1. Position the insertion point where you want the table of authorities inserted.
2. Display the References tab of the ribbon.
3. Click the Insert Table of Authorities tool in the Table of Authorities group. Word displays the Table of Authorities dialog box. (The Table of Authorities tab should be selected automatically.)

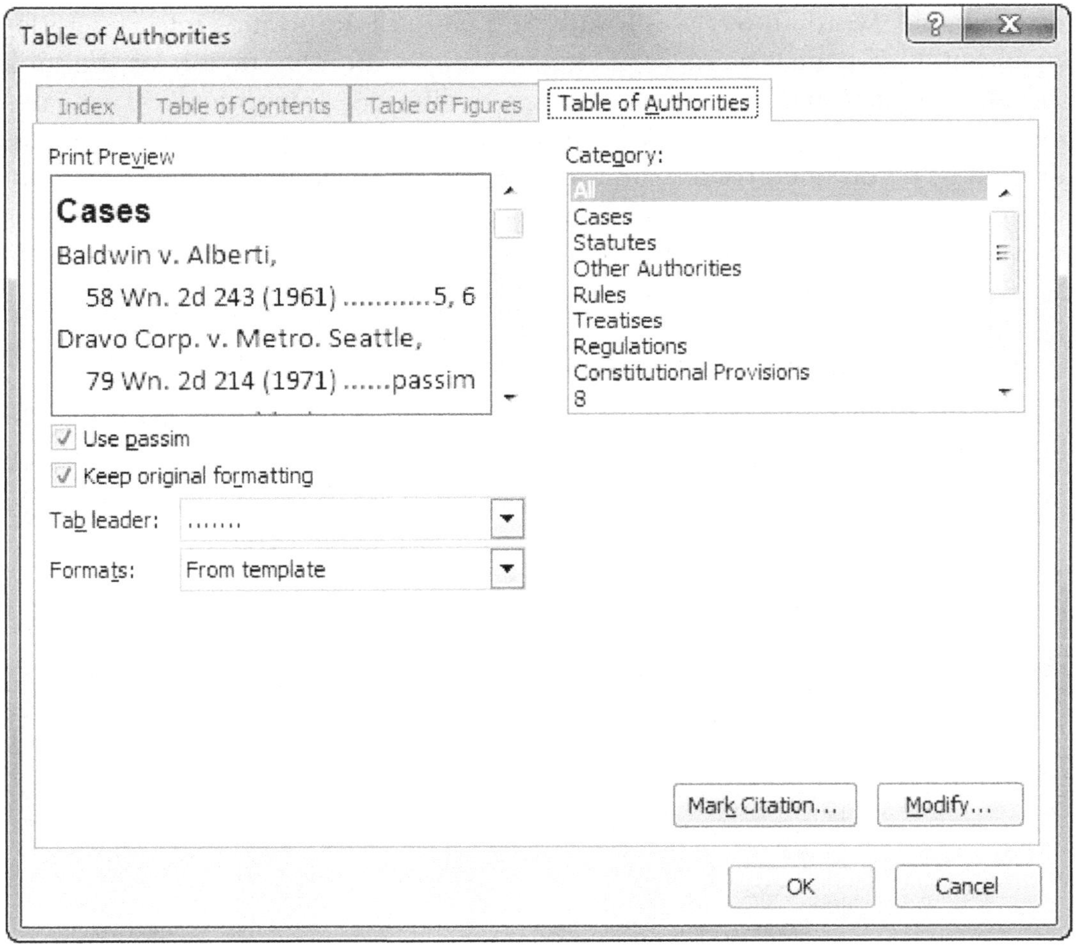

The Table of Authorities tab of the Index and Tables dialog box.

4. Pick a style in the Formats list. (If you pick the From Template choice, only the table of authorities main head is affected. It relies on the TOA Heading style.)

5. Click on OK.

Creating Categories for Your Table of Authorities

If you are developing a long legal document, a table of authorities can be very valuable. Word allows you to divide a table of authorities into categories. For instance, you may want case citations in a different section of the table than statute citations. Word provides seven different categories you can use: cases, statutes, rules, treatises, regulations, constitutional provisions, and other authorities. If you need more than these pre-defined categories, you can create your own categories. Word allows you to define up to 16 different categories, including the seven already defined. You can define your own categories by following these steps:

1. Press **Shift+Alt+I** to display the Mark Citation dialog box.
2. Click on the Categories button. (In some versions of Word it may be called the Category button.) Word displays the Edit Category dialog box.

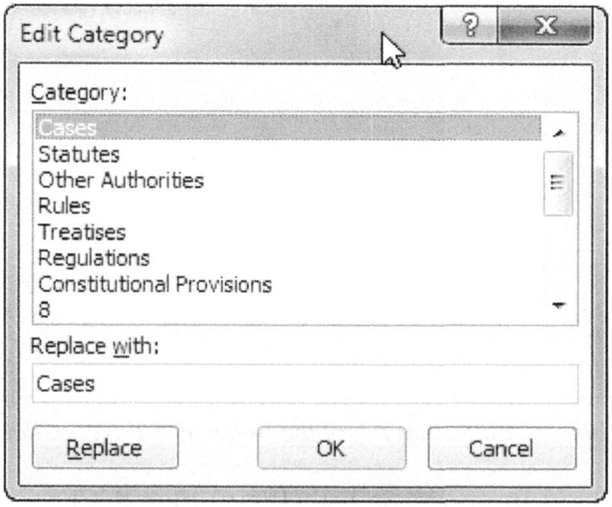

The Edit Category dialog box.

3. In the Category list, select one of the numbers, 8 through 16. (If you select one of the existing seven categories, you will end up replacing it with your new category.)
4. Edit the text in the Replace With box to reflect how you want the category to appear.
5. Click on Replace. The edited category name now appears in the Category list.
6. Click on OK.

You can now use the new category, as desired, to mark and classify citations.

Ensuring Proper Page Numbers for a Table of Authorities

Russ works with documents that require the creation of a table of authorities. In preparing a table of authorities, as you mark each cite in your document using **Alt+Shift+I**, Word inserts the resulting TA field code at the end of the cite, not the beginning. Since the location of each TA field code determines the page number that appears in the table of authorities, any cite which begins on one page and ends on the next will have the second page number in the table. Russ notes that this is incorrect, since the page number where the cite begins is the page number that should appear in the TOA. He manually moves each TA field code to the beginning of each cite as he marks it, but it would be nice not to have to do this. Russ wonders if there is any way to tell Word to place the TA field codes at the beginning of the cites as they are marked.

There are a couple of things that can be tried in this situation. First, you could change how you are adding the TA field to your cites. Instead of using **Alt+Shift+I**, paste your TA field where you want it. For instance, let's say that you have a correct TA field set up at the beginning of a cite. Select the field and copy it to the Clipboard (**Ctrl+C**). Now, position the insertion point at the beginning of the next instance of this cite and press **Ctrl+V** to paste the field in the proper location. Pressing **Ctrl+V** is just as easy as pressing **Alt+Shift+I**, and you end up with the TA field in the proper location.

Another thing you can try has to do with paragraph formatting. If the paragraphs in your document are not terribly long, you can set the formatting for the style used for the paragraphs so that a paragraph won't beak across pages. (You want to set the Keep Lines Together attribute for the style.) In this way, no paragraph will go across a page boundary and you will end up with your TA fields on the proper page all the time.

You may have also noticed that one of the optional switches for the TA field is the \r switch. This switch causes the field to reference a bookmark as the source of the page number used. You can use this \r switch as a potential solution, but the steps you go through might be just as painful as moving the TA field manually. How would you use the \r switch? If you place a bookmark at the beginning of the cite, you can reference the bookmark in the \r switch. The upshot is that regardless of where the TA field is physically located, it always refers to the location of the bookmark for the page number, and that bookmark is at the beginning of the cite.

Of course, what makes this approach painful is that the \r switch has to be added to the TA field manually, and you need to add the bookmark that the switch references. (See—I told you this could be painful.)

One thing to remember is that with some versions of Word, the TA field doesn't have to refer to just a singular place in the document. If you select the full text of the cite before adding the TA field using **Alt+Shift+I**, then the table of authorities should reference a page range if the cite breaks across two pages. In other words, it should say something like 14-15 if the cite spans the boundary between pages 14 and 15.

10

Other Special Tables

Auto Creation of an Acronym List

Karl works in an occupation that uses a lot of acronyms. Their standard procedure is to define the acronym only the first time it's used within the document. In addition, they always need to create an appendix, at the end of the document, listing the acronyms in alphabetical order along with their meanings. Karl is looking for a way to perhaps "mark" the acronym in the main body and have the acronym appendix be automatically created.

There is no way to do this directly in Word. There are several types of tables you can create automatically, such as tables of contents, tables of authorities, and indexes. These last two tables (tables of authorities and indexes) could possibly be used to create the acronym list, but only if they are not already being added to your document and only if you don't mind your acronym list including page numbers.

If you want to use the table of authorities tool in order to create an acronym list, Shauna Kelly has put together a great article on how this can be done. The article was written for earlier versions of Word, but it is still topical for doing this same task in Word 2010. It specifically talks about glossaries, which essentially what an acronym list would be.

```
http://www.ShaunaKelly.com/word/glossary/glossary.html
```

If you want to use the index tool in order to create your list, you can follow these general steps, assuming that the acronym, when defined, is followed by its meaning within parentheses:

1. Select the acronym and its meaning. This means that you find the first instance of the acronym in your document and then select that acronym along with the parenthetical meaning that follows it.
2. Press **ALT+SHIFT+X** to mark the selected text for the index.
3. Repeat steps 1 and 2 for the other acronyms you want in your list.
4. At the end of your document, insert your index. How to actually insert an index is covered elsewhere in this e-book.

You'll note that this approach leaves the parentheses in your index. If you don't want the parentheses, then you'll need to go to each acronym that you marked and display the field code used for the index. It will look something like this:

```
{ XE "abbrev (this is the definition)" }
```

Within the field code you can remove the parentheses so that the text appears just as you want it to appear in the acronym list. If you use the above method to mark only the first instance of the acronym—where it is first defined—then there will be a single page number for each acronym in your list. If you like the idea of having page numbers, but want them for all instances of each acronym, then you'll need to mark each occurrence of the acronyms—a much more involved task.

If you prefer not to use the either of the methods already described, you could create a macro to aid in creating your acronym list. The following macro essentially copies whatever text you have highlighted to the end of the document.

```
Sub Send_2_acronym_list()
    With ActiveDocument.Bookmarks
        .Add Range:=Selection.Range, Name:="xxxHERExxx"
        .DefaultSorting = wdSortByName
        .ShowHidden = True
    End With
    Selection.Copy
    Selection.EndKey Unit:=wdStory
    Selection.TypeParagraph
    Selection.PasteAndFormat (wdPasteDefault)
```

```
    Selection.GoTo What:=wdGoToBookmark, Name:="xxxHERExxx"
    Application.Run MacroName:="Normal.MoreNewMacros.EditGoTo"
    Selection.MoveRight Unit:=wdCharacter, Count:=1
End Sub
```

The idea is to select your first instance of the acronym, along with its definition, and then invoke the macro. A bookmark is set at the current location, the text is copied, the end of the document is selected, and the text added there. Then the bookmark is used so that the original location can again be selected.

When you are done "marking" your acronyms in this manner, you can select the text that was copied ot the end of the document and format it (or edit it) in any way desired.

If you want an approach that is even more automated, then you may be able to create a macro that will scan through your document and extract any acronyms it finds. In order for an approach like this to work, you'll need to make sure that you religiously follow a rigid structure for your acronyms and their definitions. The following macro assumes that the acronym will always be a string of uppercase letters followed by a space and then some parenthetical text.

```
Sub ListAcronyms()
    Dim strAcronym As String
    Dim strDefine As String
    Dim strOutput As String
    Dim newDoc As Document

    Application.ScreenUpdating = False
    Selection.HomeKey Unit:=wdStory
    ActiveWindow.View.ShowHiddenText = False

   'Loop to find all acronyms
    Do
        'Search for acronyms using wildcards
        Selection.Find.ClearFormatting
        With Selection.Find
            .ClearFormatting
            .Text = "<[A-Z]@[A-Z]>"
            .Replacement.Text = ""
            .Forward = True
            .Wrap = wdFindStop
            .Format = False
            .MatchCase = True
            .MatchWildcards = True
            .MatchWholeWord = True
            .Execute
        End With
```

```
        'Only process if something found
        If Selection.Find.Found Then
            'Make a string from the selection, add it to the
            'output string
            strAcronym = Selection.Text

            'Look for definition
            Selection.MoveRight Unit:=wdWord
            Selection.MoveRight Unit:=wdCharacter, _
              Extend:=wdExtend
            strDefine = ""
            If Selection.Text = "(" Then
                While Selection <> ")"
                    strDefine = strDefine & Selection.Text
                    Selection.Collapse Direction:=wdCollapseEnd
                    Selection.MoveRight Unit:=wdCharacter, _
                      Extend:=wdExtend
                Wend
            End If
            Selection.Collapse Direction:=wdCollapseEnd
            If Left(strDefine, 1) = "(" Then
                strDefine = Mid(strDefine, 2, Len(strDefine))
            End If
            If strDefine > "" Then
                'Check if the search result is in the Output string
                'if it is, ignore the search result
                If InStr(strOutput, strAcronym) = 0 Then
                    strOutput = strOutput & strAcronym _
                      & vbTab & strDefine & vbCr
                End If
            End If
        End If
    Loop Until Not Selection.Find.Found

    'Create new document and change active document
    Set newDoc = Documents.Add

    'Insert the text
    Selection.TypeText Text:=strOutput

    'Sort it
    newDoc.Content.Sort SortOrder:=wdSortOrderAscending
    Application.ScreenUpdating = True
    Selection.HomeKey Unit:=wdStory
End Sub
```

The macro looks through the document for anything it thinks might be an acronym. If it finds a candidate, it looks after it to see if it is followed by an opening parenthesis. If so, then everything up to the closing parenthesis is considered the definition for the acronym. Once the macro is finished going through the document, it creates a new document, adds the acronyms there, and then sorts them all.

Creating Usable Figure Captions

Ron wondered how to use figure captions with images inserted in a text box. The captions are inserted OK, but they are not available as cross-references or for inclusion in a Table of Figures.

This, unfortunately, is a shortcoming of Word when it comes to text boxes. The first problem (not being able to use the captions in cross-references) can be overcome with a bit of ingenuity. Simply bookmark the caption, then cross-reference the bookmark within text. This extra step can get to be a bother, however.

The best solution if you really need cross-references and Table of Figures inclusion is to not insert your figures in text boxes. Instead, insert them in old-fashioned frames. Frames have been fully described in other issues of ***WordTips.*** They are similar to text boxes, but there are some subtle-yet-important differences that can make them the option of choice, at times. One of those differences is that when you insert a figure and caption into a frame, the caption is available both for cross-referencing and for inclusion in a Table of Figures.

The reason for this difference is where Word tracks the different elements. A text box is considered part of the Drawing layer, not a part of the document itself. As such, text boxes are not referenced in some features of Word. Frames, on the other hand, are a part of the Document layer, and fully available to the required features.

Turning Off Figure Caption Numbering

Bill wants to label the figures in his document with captions. He knows that Word can create figure captions, but it always seems to number the captions. Bill doesn't want to include a number; he just wants the caption that he specifies for the figure. So he wonders if there is a way to turn off the figure caption numbering.

Word, indeed, does not allow you to turn off caption numbering and still use the automatic captioning feature. You can, however, use the feature to add numbered captions and later edit each caption to remove the numbers.

This is probably more work than you want to do, however. A quicker way is to just add your own captions to each figure manually. Type the caption (you'd have to do that in the captioning feature anyway) and then use either the built-in Caption style or your own custom style to control how the caption looks. If you need a way to refer to the caption in your main text, you can then define a bookmark that encompasses the caption and reference that bookmark in the text.

One of the benefits of using the automatic captioning feature, of course, is that your captions can be gathered together by Word and placed in a table of figures. This can't be done quite as easily if you use your own manual captions. However, if you are careful to use a single style to format your captions, you can modify the way that Word pulls together the TOF to make sure that all paragraphs with that particular style are included. (How you do this has been covered in other *WordTips*.)

Overriding Automatic Numbering of Tables

Chris has a document with tables. She wants two TOCs, one for the document and one for the tables. The tables are labeled 1, 2, 3, etc., but then she added some tables like 16A, 16B, and 17A. When Chris updates the TOC for the tables, Word changes her table numbers, such as changing 16B to 17 and 17A to 18. Chris wonders if there is a way to override Word so the TOC will list the tables with the letters after the number.

If you are using Word's automatic number, it is intended to sequentially number items, pure and simple. Word would have no way of knowing where "deviations" should occur, such as with tables 16A, 16B, and 17A. While you can try to make the changes in the document itself, the moment Word updates the numbering your alterations will be "renumbered" to again be sequential.

Your best bet is to number the tables manually, using whatever style you want for the table caption that contains the number. For instance, you might use a paragraph style called MyTables for the captions. You can then create a TOC for your tables that gathers only the paragraphs formatted using the MyTables style. (How to create a TOC that references a particular style is covered in the next tip.) The individual table numbers, since they are manual, could appear using any type of numbering you desired.

Table Numbers are Skipped

Geoff has a Word document with about 40 numbered tables. In a few places throughout the document the table numbering breaks down. For example, the table numbers will skip a number, e.g. Table 16, Table 17, then Table 19. The cross referencing also goes wrong, and the table list in the table of contents is wrong. Geoff has updated fields throughout the document and re-inserted the table captions, but to no avail.

There are no clear-cut answers as to why this problem could be happening, but there are a few things you can try. First, you should check the styles used for the captions. Make sure that there are no inconsistencies in the styles used (at either a paragraph or character level), as this could cause Word to throw off the number under some circumstances.

Next, check the actual fields used for the table captions. Display the field codes (press **Alt+F9**) and compare them to make sure that they, too, are consistent with each other.

Also check to make sure that hidden text is displayed in your document. It could be that the missing caption is there, but is marked as hidden text and therefore not displayed. You can display the hidden text by displaying the Word Options dialog box and using the controls accessible when you click Display at the left side of the dialog box.

If you've been using Track Changes in the document, it is also possible that the missing caption was accidentally deleted, but Word still treats it as if it is there for numbering purposes. Make sure Track Changes is turned off, and then use the controls on the Review tab of the ribbon to accept all the changes in the document. Refresh the fields, and hopefully your missing caption number will reappear.

Finally, if none of the above work, you should consider the possibility that the document is somehow corrupted. (Document corruption can manifest itself in a variety of ways.) Open a new, blank document, and then select the entire original document except the final paragraph mark. (Excluding this final paragraph mark is very important.) Press **Ctrl+C**, go back to the blank document, then press **Ctrl+V**. Check to see, in the new document, if the numbering is corrected.

Made in the USA
Monee, IL
08 November 2026

67816247R00057